STABILIZATION POLICY IN AN AFRICAN SETTING

D0417282

Studies in the Economics of Africa
Editors: I. LIVINGSTONE and H. W. ORD

Stabilization Policy in an African Setting

KENYA 1963–1973

J. R. KING
Formerly Lecturer in Economics
University of Nairobi

LONDON
HEINEMANN
NAIROBI · IBADAN · LUSAKA

Heinemann Educational Books Ltd
48 Charles Street, London WIX 8AH
P.M.B. 5205 Ibadan · P.O. Box 45314 Nairobi
P.O. Box 3966 Lusaka
EDINBURGH MELBOURNE TORONTO AUCKLAND KINGSTON
SINGAPORE HONG KONG KUALA LUMPUR NEW DELHI
Heinemann Educational Books Inc
4 Front Street, Exeter, New Hampshire 03833

ISBN 0 435 97375 4 (cased)
      0 435 97376 2 (paper)

Text set in 10/11 pt Photon Times, printed by photolithography,
and bound in Great Britain at The Pitman Press, Bath

Contents

Acknowledgements

Many people have contributed to the writing of this book, and I should like to thank them all. My greatest debts are to my wife Anne for unfaltering encouragement and confidence that the enterprise would be finished; to my former colleagues in the Universities of Nairobi and Lancaster for the stimulus of their example and criticism while the ideas presented in this book were taking shape; and in particular to Walter Elkan, Tony Killick and Alasdair MacBean, and to the Editors of this series, for painstaking comments on earlier drafts. None of these can escape some responsibility, and my gratitude, for the fact that the study was completed; but they are not to be blamed for the conclusions which it reaches, or for any errors or obscurities which it still contains.

The argument of the book was completed before I took up my present duties as an economist in the Inland Revenue. The opinions which it expresses are my own: they should not be interpreted, in any respect, as a reflection of the views of the British Civil Service.

J. R. KING

List of Tables

List of Figures

Preface

This book is an argument about the teaching of an important area of economics – namely, that part which deals with the behaviour of national economies in what is conventionally described as the 'short run'. It is about prices, unemployment and the balance of payments, and how they may be influenced or controlled by government policies.

In writing it, my main concern has been the needs of students of economics in the English-speaking countries of Africa. For this reason the book contains a certain amount of exposition, and I hope that it will be useful in the teaching of economics. But it is an argument, not a textbook; it seeks to widen the horizons of the student rather than take the place of existing textbooks. Indeed, it assumes on the reader's behalf a knowledge of what is currently taught in A-level courses, or in first year university courses in economics in the English-speaking world.

The book's origins lie in the dissatisfaction which I felt as a teacher of economics, first in Mauritius, then in Kenya and most recently in Britain, with the way in which the student has been introduced in recent years to the economics of stabilization policy. This conventional introduction is based upon a simple model of an economy (often referred to as the 'income–expenditure model') which was introduced into the economic literature in the 1940s as a distillation of the most important ideas in J. M. Keynes's *The General Theory of Employment, Interest and Money.*

As a vehicle of exposition the income–expenditure model has a number of weaknesses. First, it leaves out a good many things which it is generally felt that the student of economics must learn about – for example, the operations of the monetary system and of commercial banks. For the beginning student it is often difficult to see where these extra bits and pieces fit in to the overall framework. Second, the income–expenditure model makes a very large number of rather extreme assumptions about the way that individual households and firms behave. What these assumptions are, and how seriously the model's implications are changed when they are made more realistic, are matters which become clear only to someone who pursues the study of economics to degree level or beyond. The teacher is obliged by the income–expenditure model to sweep some serious difficulties under the carpet, and to hope that not too many students will notice.

Now, it may be argued that these familiar weaknesses are unavoidable: the teaching of stabilization policy must start somewhere, and it is inevitable that its starting-point should be a model which is both incomplete and question-begging. The justification for using the income–expenditure model is therefore simply that it is the best vehicle available for providing the student with a quick understanding of the important macroeconomic relationships which operate in the real world.

I argue in this book that this justification will not do. In the first place there is an alternative model which provides a more comprehensive picture of an economy, begs fewer questions, yet which is no less simple than the income–expenditure model. This alternative model is what is currently described in the economic literature as the 'monetary theory of the balance of payments'. In the second place, the latter model provides a much closer approximation to the important macroeconomic relationships in those economies with which I am familiar than does the income–expenditure model. What this book attempts to do, therefore, is to try to persuade the reader to compare the income–expenditure model (with which I assume he is familiar) with the monetary theory of the balance of payments, and to compare both these models with the real world.

The book is in two main parts. The first part is about general ideas, theories and schools of thought in economics. Chapter 1 is about stabilization policy – what the term means, and what distinguishes this area of economics from other areas of the subject. Chapter 2 is a brief exposition of particular versions of the two models which are the subject of the book. Chapter 3 then relates these two theoretical models to some past and present areas of public controversy between different schools of thought on the subject of stabilization policy.

The second part of the book is a case study of a single economy, Kenya, in its first ten years as an independent country from 1963 to 1973. Chapter 4 describes the conduct of stabilization policy in Kenya in this period. Chapter 5 compares the ability of the two simple models to explain Kenya's experience, argues that the 'monetary' framework is to be preferred, and constructs a simple model of the Kenyan economy based upon this framework. Chapter 6 then puts this model of the Kenyan economy to work, illustrating the lessons that can be drawn from it about the way in which government policies affected the economy in the period covered by the case study. This provides the basis for the final chapter of the book where it is argued, in the Kenyan context, that the choice of model in the teaching of stabilization policy is a matter of more than mere academic importance: the way in which economics is taught, I suggest, has a powerful effect upon the decisions that economic policy makers arrive at, and so upon the way that economies in the real world behave.

Every economy in the modern world is unique, and the sceptical reader may perhaps feel that Kenya's special characteristics make it unrepresentative as a case study. Starting from an extremely low level of *per capita* income on the eve of independence in 1963, heavily dependent upon a variety of agricultural exports (mainly coffee, tea, sisal and pyrethrum) and upon expatriate communities of Asians and Europeans for its skills, it grew rapidly in the first ten years of independence. Government development expenditures, foreign investment on a major scale – both government and private – and the opening up of new opportunities in industries such as tourism were major engines of growth. But for an outside observer, the most striking aspect of change in Kenya in this period was the way in which a colonial economy ruled by an expatriate élite was transformed into a flourishing, confident, national economy by the efforts of its own peoples. With the exception of those countries which were able to exploit mineral wealth or fossil fuels, Kenya was among the fastest-growing economies in the world in the late 1960s and early 1970s.

None of this suggests that Kenya is an unsuitable country to choose as a case-study of the relevance of the argument presented in this book. But four characteristics of the economy *are* relevant, and deserve a mention here. First, the economy is a very 'open' one, with exports accounting for one-quarter or more of domestic production and imports for a rather greater proportion of domestic expenditure. Second, the Kenyan economy was and remains a 'mixed' one, with the public sector concentrating mainly on administration and infrastructure, and with a high proportion of 'productive' activity in private hands. Third, despite rapid industrial growth in the period covered by this study, Kenya remains predominantly an agricultural and trading economy. Finally, since the local capital market is still rather small, Kenya receives very little portfolio investment from overseas (as distinct from direct investment), and its currency is not used to a significant extent as a trading medium by other countries. These characteristics have an important bearing upon the assumptions which it is appropriate to make in a model of the way in which the economy behaves; to the extent that they are not shared by other economies, the argument that I develop in the Kenyan context might need qualification elsewhere.

When I began to write this book some years ago I was afraid that its conclusions about the Kenyan economy might strike many of my colleagues as rather radical. But fashions are changing: the 1970s have witnessed a remarkable resurgence of interest in the monetary theory of the balance of payments and awareness of its implications (particularly in those countries, such as Kenya and the UK, which have been obliged to turn to the International Monetary Fund for balance of payments support). This change is beginning to have an effect upon the teaching of economics. But it is still true that the monetary theory of the balance of payments is encountered only at an advanced level of economics teaching. What this book attempts to do is to make it accessible, in a simple form, to a wider audience.

Part 1

STABILIZATION POLICY: A BUNDLE OF IDEAS

It is, I think, of the essential nature of economic exposition that it gives ... a sample statement, so to speak, out of all the things which could be said, intended to suggest to the reader the whole bundle of ideas, so that, if he catches the bundle, he will not in the least be confused or impeded by the technical incompleteness of the mere words which the author has written down.

J. M. Keynes[1]

1 *Objectives and Instruments of Stabilization Policy*

A stabilization policy means more than just ironing out fluctuations at a particular level: instead, the policy is essentially short run macroeconomic policy aimed at such things as a high level of employment, some sort of target for the behaviour of the price level, and in an open economy some attention to the balance of payments as well.

attributed to R. M. Solow

1.1 THE MEANING OF 'STABILIZATION POLICY'

Stabilization policy is a technical term in the language of economics. Technical terms are often thought to require precise definition. In fact, however, one very rarely finds this particular term defined at all, even in an approximate manner. The rough attempt which is reproduced at the beginning of this chapter is one of the few exceptions to this generalization to be found in the literature. And even this exception is to be found in the report of an oral debate, rather than in written work by its author.[2]

But the absence of a standard, precise definition does not normally prove to be a source of confusion. I have no fear that an economist who perseveres to the end of this book will feel that he was misled by its title. What accounts, then, for our inability or unwillingness to define the term precisely?

The answer is that its function in economic discourse is to call to mind what J. M. Keynes described as a 'bundle of ideas', about some particular concerns and instruments of public policy. Many of these ideas are objects of continuing refinement and debate. New ideas are occasionally added to the bundle; less frequently perhaps, old ones disappear from it. So its contents are neither distinct nor fixed. Nevertheless at any time there is a common thread running through these ideas, uniting them as a distinctive set which may conveniently be called to mind by a single family name.

This common thread is a theoretical tradition. Its origins may be traced far back in the history of economic ideas. But contemporary western economists usually trace its origins in their modern form to the publication in 1936 of

Keynes's book *The General Theory of Employment, Interest and Money*. As the student of economics learns the ideas of Keynes from textbooks, he comes to grasp the essence of what is meant by stabilization policy in contemporary economic discourse. It is sometimes helpful to have a concise reminder such as Solow's, which defines stabilization policy in terms of its instruments ('short run macroeconomic policy') and its characteristic concerns or objectives (employment, the price level and the balance of payments). But the essential meaning of the term is to be found in the theoretical tradition which links these instruments and objectives.

This book will have a good deal to say about *The General Theory* and the 'Keynesian revolution' in economic thinking which followed its publication; and much of what it says, particularly about the latter, will be rather critical. For this reason it is necessary to be more than usually precise about the particular objectives and instruments of policy upon which the discussion will focus.

1.2   OBJECTIVES OF STABILIZATION POLICY

The three practical concerns of government policy that are to be examined are the level of economic activity, the rate of inflation and the balance of payments.

1.21   *The Level of Economic Activity*

The term economic activity has been chosen for the first objective in preference to equivalent terms such as output or employment.

Keynes preferred to describe this same objective as the level of employment. He did so for reasons which can best be understood in a historical context. At the time when he was writing *The General Theory* and indeed for many years previously, several million people in Britain were without any means of supporting themselves or their families, apart from a meagre payment which was distributed by the government. Similar conditions prevailed throughout most of Western Europe and North America. The total number of people who were 'unemployed' in this particular sense was one of the few meaningful macroeconomic statistics which were regularly published at the time. It pointed an accusing finger at an economic system which could tolerate such waste of manpower, and the poverty and degradation which it inflicted upon individuals, for years at a stretch. Throughout the 1920s and 1930s Keynes devoted the major part of his energies in theorizing and in polemic to making possible an improvement in the social conditions which were reflected in the published unemployment statistics. Employment and unemployment were his fundamental concern.

But theoretical work does require precise definitions, and Keynes was especially careful about the ones that he chose. In *The General Theory*, he defined in the following terms the unemployment whose persistence and remedy he sought to explain:

> Men are involuntarily unemployed if, in the event of a small rise in the price of wage–goods relatively to the money wage, both the aggregate supply of labour willing to work for the current money wage and the aggregate demand for it at that wage would be greater than the existing volume of employment.[3]

For economists who have been brought up on textbook simplifications, the language of *The General Theory* sometimes seems to be almost wilfully obscure. One eminent (and eminently readable) modern economist, J. K. Galbraith, has even complained about the book's 'almost unique illegibility'.[4] But in this instance there were good reasons for the complexity of Keynes's definition of involuntary unemployment, and the preference of economists for simpler alternatives has sometimes led to confusion.

These reasons can be understood fully only after a detailed examination of the economic model which was sketched in *The General Theory* – a task which lies outside the scope of this book. But two important points about Keynes's involuntary unemployment (which will be referred to as KIU for short and to emphasize its individuality) may be noted even in a brief inspection of its definition.

In the first place KIU is not simply a matter of 'labour' being willing to work at the going wage rate but unable to find employment, and still less is it just a matter of *workers* being in this position. Instead, for KIU to be known to exist, it is necessary in principle that employment for labour should be forthcoming, in circumstances which Keynes chose to specify rather carefully. It follows from this that if one wants to know whether or not KIU exists in an economy at a particular point in time, it is not enough to examine the circumstances of any group of workers, or of the labour market as a whole. Labour market indicators may well reflect the presence of KIU, as Keynes believed they did in Britain in the 1930s; but they can never *demonstrate* its presence.

Second, the definition offers no guidance at all about how the extent of KIU might be measured – except perhaps in retrospect, once 'a small rise in the price of wage–goods relatively to the money wage' has taken place, and its effect upon the employment of 'labour' can be studied with the wisdom of hindsight. This is potentially rather awkward for policy makers, because if they are to try to control or influence the extent of KIU they need to be able to measure it.

Since the 1940s most governments in Western Europe and North America have made what amounts to a leap of faith in using labour force statistics as if they are an indicator of KIU and nothing else of any significance. In some countries, such as the USA, the statistics are derived from regular sample surveys of the labour force as a whole. In others, such as Britain, they are based upon individual registrations at government employment exchanges. In its early years the habit of using such statistics as a practical measure of KIU undoubtedly had the sanction of Keynes himself, but it did not have the logical sanction of Keynes's theory. The usefulness of labour market surveys and employment exchange registrations as indicators of KIU has therefore proved to be a matter of debate, in different circumstances.

In most developing countries, where such statistics have been collected on an increasing scale since the beginning of the 1950s, the debate has usually been resolved very quickly. In such countries it is now agreed by almost all economists that the available labour market statistics reflect so many features of the economy besides the extent of KIU, that their value as a practical indicator of the latter is minimal.

In Europe and America the present position is rather less clear cut. It seems fair to say that an increasing number of economists in these areas treat labour market statistics with reservations or positive suspicion when searching for evidence about the behaviour of KIU. But 'an increasing number' does not mean a consensus, or even a majority. And in practice such statistics continue to be used for this purpose by governments and economic commentators: for one does not give up without a struggle an indicator which has been relied upon in the past as a guide to policy, when the policies based upon its behaviour have not proved obviously absurd. An active debate is therefore still in progress.

Now, for such a debate to be possible at all it is necessary that alternative measures of KIU should be available, at least in principle, and indeed they are. For in the model which Keynes sketched in *The General Theory*, KIU is related inversely to employment and nothing else; and employment is made a simple positive function of output (or if one is to be strictly accurate, the output of 'wage-goods': but in this instance the simpler terminology may be used without serious distortion). So Keynes's theory of employment and unemployment was essentially a theory about how an economy's output could remain below an attainable level, at which KIU would be zero. If this 'full employment' level of output could be estimated, the gap between it and an economy's actual output would provide a simple measure of the extent of KIU. (The measure would not be a linear one, but the relationship between it and KIU would be strictly positive.)

A common approach to measuring the full employment output level at different points in time has been to begin by assuming that it will change only gradually, on the grounds that it depends basically upon the stock of resources in the economy and upon the state of technology, each of which will be subject only to gradual change. The growth rate of full employment output may then be roughly estimated from the trend growth rate of actual output, or from the average growth rate of output between the peak of one cycle and the next. An assumption that output was at, or near to, its full employment level at just one point in the past then makes it possible for an absolute figure to be attached to full employment output at every other point in time.

This sort of method may legitimately be criticized as unsatisfactory, because it is based upon untestable assumptions about the variable which it is being used to measure. But many economists have come to the view that such methods, when used with discretion, can provide more satisfactory estimates of the extent of KIU than any available labour market statistics, even in countries such as the

USA and the UK.

There is however one important practical difficulty which must be mentioned. An economy's actual output and its full employment level may both be affected by a number of random factors, such as the weather and natural or unnatural disasters. An estimate of the extent of KIU which is to be based upon the behaviour of actual output must take account of such factors, which are likely to have a particularly important effect upon output in predominantly agricultural economies. It seems preferable, then, that the output statistics which one uses for this purpose should in general exclude the output of the agricultural sector, and any other sectors of an economy which are likely to be seriously affected by similar random factors. To avoid confusion, therefore, it is useful to describe the object of concern by a rather vaguer phrase than 'the level of output', at least in empirical work. 'The level of economic activity' is an appropriate substitute.

As the term is used in this book, therefore, the level of economic activity is a measure of the extent to which an economy's actual output in a particular period of time approximates an attainable full employment level at which KIU, as defined by Keynes, would be zero. It is perhaps most convenient to think of economic activity as being measured on a percentage scale, with 100 per cent corresponding to full employment. But the units of measurement are arbitrary. The important point in the choice of terminology here is simply to make it clear that this book will neglect – as Keynes did – those many aspects of employment and unemployment, as measured by different kinds of labour market statistics, which are not a concern of stabilization policy. This is a particularly important point to make in a study of Kenya, because this economy is generally regarded as suffering from serious problems of employment and unemployment: but, as these problems have recently been analysed, they do not include a substantial element of KIU.[5]

1.22 *The Rate of Inflation*

The term inflation is sometimes used to refer to a rise in the general level of prices in an economy, and sometimes to refer to one of several things which are believed by different schools of thought to cause such a rise in prices – for example an increase in the stock of money, or a level of aggregate demand for goods and services which exceeds the full employment level of economic activity. Because later chapters will compare different theories about how the level of prices is determined, it is rather important that our terminology should not beg any questions about which theory is the most appropriate one. In this book, therefore, the term inflation is used to refer to a rise in the general level of prices, irrespective of its causes.

The general level of prices in an economy may appear to be a straightforward concept, but it is not. Something must be said here about two important problems which it raises.

In the first place, it is an average of the prices paid in a very large number of individual transactions in any period of time that may be chosen. If the set of transactions taking place in an economy was the same in each period of time, it would be possible to devise a single, appropriate method of calculating an average of their prices. But in practice, of course, the set of transactions never does stay constant. Not only does the relative importance of different transactions change, but new kinds of goods and services are constantly being introduced and old ones are disappearing. This means there is not one 'correct' way in which an average should be calculated. Indices of this average which have been constructed in different ways will tell different stories about the behaviour of the general level of prices in a single economy, and none can claim to tell the 'right' story. There is therefore an unavoidable element of ambiguity in the concept of a general price level.

Modern economists usually consider this ambiguity to be of minor significance, and are happy both to make use of the concept of a general price level and to measure its changes over time with an index number. But this is a relatively recent development in economics. It was precisely because earlier generations were aware of the ambiguity that they did not begin to calculate indices of general price levels until the second half of the nineteenth century. And the same awareness probably helps to explain why the theories to account for general price movements which had been developed in the seventeenth and eighteenth centuries were never set down in a very precise way. (Of course, the lack of the tools provided by modern algebra is an important part of the explanation too.)

Until these inhibitions were overcome, formal macroeconomic theorizing could not begin. For the same ambiguity is present in the concept of a level of output, to which we are already committed. Given any set of transactions between money and various different kinds of goods and services, one can measure without any ambiguity at all the total value of goods and services exchanged in terms of money. But to measure either the total volume of goods and services or the average price at which they change hands, an index number is needed; and once one has provided an index number as a measure of one of these things, one has automatically provided an index number as a measure of the other. The problem of ambiguity which is raised by the concept of an aggregate level of output is therefore not only similar in kind to that raised by the concept of a general level of prices – it is exactly the same problem. The two concepts must stand or fall together. In this book they are both allowed to stand, for the practical reason that they are indispensable in formal theorizing about economic stabilization, and in the empirical application of such theories.

The second problem which is raised by the concept of a general level of prices can be dealt with rather more satisfactorily. This problem concerns the choice of a set of transactions over which prices are to be averaged. In the closed economy with which most textbooks begin, all sales made by domestic residents are simultaneously sales to domestic residents. In these circumstances it would make no difference whether one based an average upon the prices of domestic purchases or upon the prices of domestic sales, since the two would exactly coincide. But in an economy which engages in foreign trade, as all national economies in the modern world do to a greater or lesser extent, the coincidence ceases to be exact. It is then important to be clear whether one's average of domestic prices is an average over transactions in which domestic residents are acting as buyers or as sellers.

Because governments' concern about inflation usually stems from worries about the prices which residents have to pay as consumers rather than about the prices which they receive as producers, it seems preferable to use the term 'the general level of prices' to refer to an index of prices in transactions in which domestic residents act as buyers. As a rule, this is the concept which is employed in the chapters which follow. It will occasionally be necessary, however, for the reader to be reminded of the distinction between these two alternative concepts.

To summarize: in this book 'the rate of inflation' means the rate of increase of an appropriate index of prices paid in transactions in which domestic residents act as buyers of goods and services.

1.23 The Balance of Payments

Each of the first two concerns of stabilization policy can be measured by a single figure. The original meaning of the phrase 'the balance of payments' was also a single figure, which could in principle be measured precisely and unambiguously. In the seventeenth and eighteenth centuries the balance of payments meant the excess of an economy's immediate claims on foreign countries over its immediate obligations to foreign countries, arising from transactions in any particular time period. This balance had to be liquidated by movements of gold and silver 'specie', and it could therefore be measured straightforwardly by the value of these movements.

But as the international financial system has developed, national moneys and various forms of credit have increasingly replaced specie as the medium of exchange in international transactions. This development has made it difficult for many countries, especially those whose national money is used in settlement of international debts, to preserve in their statistics a single measure of 'overall balance' which corresponds in altered circumstances to what was originally meant by the phrase.

The USA provides the clearest example of this difficulty. In recent years its government has dealt with the problem by providing several alternative measures of overall balance, among which the user of its statistics is invited to choose for himself. And it is about to go one step further, suggesting no measures at all but instead providing enough detailed information to enable the user of its statistics to construct a wide variety of possible measures according to his tastes. The USA is perhaps an extreme case, but it illustrates an important general point: when the phrase 'the balance of payments' is used by modern economists to refer to a single total, the appropriate way to measure that total may vary widely between different countries. And this variety has undoubtedly contributed to a further development in the terminology of economics: the balance of payments now frequently means not a single total, but rather the entire set of accounts describing a country's international transactions in a particular period of time.

However, for a country such as Kenya whose domestic money is not used on any substantial scale in international transactions, it is still possible to provide a simple measure of overall balance which corresponds quite closely to the original meaning of the term. This measure is the change in any period of time in the domestic monetary system's claims upon foreign countries. As a concern of government policy, it is this total which will be referred to in this book as a country's balance of payments.

But it will also be convenient for us to use the phrase from time to time in its wider sense, to refer to a country's international transactions as a whole, classified into the following broad categories:

(i) *the current account* (covering an economy's transactions with others in goods and services);

(ii) *the capital account* (covering transactions in claims upon future goods and services, excluding those made by an economy's monetary system); and

(iii) *monetary movements* (which is the balance of payments in its stricter sense, already defined).

The sum of the separate balances on these three accounts should by definition equal zero. In order to ensure that it does so in practice, it is convenient to assume at this stage that any transactions which cannot be placed straight-forwardly in one or other of these three rough categories – for example, unilateral transfers between individuals or governments – are to be included in the capital account.

These various definitions are very rough ones indeed, but they are sufficiently precise for the purposes of the next few chapters. When exact definitions are needed for empirical purposes later in the book, they will be borrowed with minor modifications from those which are used in practice by Kenya's government statisticians.

1.3   SOME OTHER OBJECTIVES OF POLICY

The previous section described the three characteristic concerns of stabilization policy. The common factor which unites them in the minds of modern economists is, it was suggested, a theoretical tradition. It is certainly not their importance in the minds of either economists or policy makers. Indeed there are many other concerns of economic policy, such as the distribution of income and wealth and the rate of economic growth, which governments are likely to consider very much more important. It is useful to digress briefly to examine some of these other objectives, because in doing so one can learn a good deal about the theoretical tradition which sets the objectives of stabilization policy apart as a distinctive group.

1.31 *The Distribution of Incomes*

The distribution of incomes has been of interest to economists since the early years of the discipline. Indeed for many, such as David Ricardo in the early years of the nineteenth century, it has seemed the most important and interesting aspect of a society that economics can shed light upon.

There is to be found in the work of classical economists such as Ricardo an account of how, in the ordinary course of events, income will be distributed between three aggregate factors of production labelled 'land', 'labour' and 'capital'. In its Marxist variant, this theory has of course been of dramatic ideological and political significance in the twentieth century. Governments whose concern about income distribution extends only to the distribution between the three 'classes' which 'own' these factors of production can look to the theories of Ricardo, Marx and their successors for useful analytical assistance in the pursuit of their objectives.

Marx believed that in the course of time there would be a tendency for households to fall into three relatively homogeneous groups in a capitalist economy, with each group deriving its income from the sale of just one factor. If this was so, a concern about the distribution of income between *households* and a concern about the 'functional' distribution between *factors* would amount to the same thing. But it is difficult to hold Marx's belief without qualification, in the face of empirical evidence which has subsequently accumulated. It is perfectly possible and not uncommon for the share of 'labour' in the national income of a country to rise, and yet for the degree of income inequality between households (according to a variety of possible measures of this multidimensional concept) to worsen; and the converse is also true. In practice the factors of production are very far from being homogeneous, and most households – both poor and rich – continue to 'own' some combination of the three factors.

If this position is accepted, it follows that economists cannot provide much practical insight into what determines the distribution of income between *households* so long as the actors in their economic models are simple undifferentiated categories such as Consumers and Firms, or even Workers, Rentiers and Capitalists. To deal adequately with this area of concern, models with a much finer texture are required. By contrast, there is no difficulty in principle about using models of a coarse and simple texture to analyse the behaviour of aggregate variables such as economic activity, inflation and the balance of payments, and this is indeed the usual practice of contemporary economists.

So what sets the distribution of income apart is essentially a matter of the kind of theoretical model which economists generally use to account for its behaviour. Economic activity, inflation and the balance of payments are approached with macroeconomic models; but this kind of model can provide at best an insight into the functional distribution of income, which is only one among many aspects of the problem of income distribution.

It is important to note however that although the distribution of income is not one of the characteristic concerns of stabilization policy, it is closely related to them. For if one enquires why governments set themselves particular objectives for economic activity or inflation, the answer in practice often seems to be that these variables are connected to the way in which income is distributed: KIU and inflation hurt particular groups of households, and benefit others. And governments' choices between the various instruments which can be used to stabilize an economy are also strongly influenced in practice by who will gain and who will lose from the use of these instruments.

1.32   *The Rate of Economic Growth*

The rate of growth of output, like the level of output or economic activity, is clearly an entirely suitable variable for inclusion in a macroeconomic model. But it is set apart from the three characteristic concerns of stabilization policy by the fact that it is essentially a concern of long run rather than short run policy, in the technical sense in which these terms are used in economics.

An increase in output can occur in two distinct ways. Either economic activity can increase, without any change in an economy's full employment level of output; or the full employment level of output can itself increase. What one sees when one measures a particular economy's growth rate in practice will be some combination of these two things. But it is potentially confusing to include both of them in what is meant by economic growth, as an objective of policy; for the first has already appeared in our list of concerns of stabilization policy. In the interests of clarity it is therefore desirable that the term economic growth should be confined, among policy objectives, to the second – that is, to an increase in an economy's full employment output level.

So if economists are to consider growth as an objective of policy, and develop models to assist governments in pursuing it, these models must include the full employment output level as an 'endogenous' variable, determined by the other variables in the system. By contrast, it is possible to treat economic activity, inflation and the balance of payments using short run models in which the full employment output level is assumed to be determined 'exogenously', that is to say outside the system under consideration.

Now this may seem a minor point, because it is a relatively straightforward matter technically to modify a short run macroeconomic model in such a way as to make the full employment output level an endogenously determined variable. But although it is easy for a model-builder to do this, it is at present very difficult indeed to do it in such a way as to account plausibly for what is known about variations and differences in national economic growth rates in the real world. If anything certain has emerged from the large amount of empirical work on economic growth which has been undertaken during the last twenty years or so, it is that the determinants of the growth rate of full employment output are many and complex. So although simple macroeconomic growth models are a lively and important area of theoretical development in economics, they have not yet proved of much value to policy makers who are concerned to influence their economies' rates of growth.

This point may be put in more down-to-earth terms: if one asks why the full employment level of output in Kenya's monetary economy should have grown between 1963 and 1973, in so far as one can judge, at an annual rate of 7.5 per cent rather than 5 per cent or 10 per cent, only a rash economist would give a confident answer; but it will be argued in this book that the behaviour of economic activity, prices and the balance of payments in Kenya in these years can be accounted for reasonably completely and with some confidence.

1.4 INSTRUMENTS OF STABILIZATION POLICY

The main instruments with which we shall be concerned in this book are aggregate fiscal and monetary policies, and exchange rate policy. Various forms of administrative controls over prices and the balance of payments will also make an appearance. But when they do so, they will appear as minor characters, for such controls are not usually treated as a characteristic element of stabilization policy. And there is a good reason for this, a reason which has nothing to do with the author's prejudices about which instruments *should* be used to control an economy: to the extent that the concerns of policy can be controlled by simple administrative methods, one does not require a macroeconomic model to account for the relationship between instruments and objectives.

1.41 *Aggregate Fiscal Policy*

The term aggregate fiscal policy will be used to refer to decisions about the level of government expenditures, and the way in which the necessary finance is to be derived from different broad categories of government revenue (in particular taxation, foreign borrowing and grants, borrowing from domestic residents, and borrowing from the domestic monetary system). These are decisions which governments must necessarily reach in their regular budgetary exercises, and so the term budgetary policy is an equally suitable one with which to refer to them.

There is an important distinction to be drawn between what governments decide and what they actually do, because different decisions must be implemented in different ways. The level of government expenditures, for example, is usually for the most part under the direct control of the fiscal authorities. But this tends to be less true of the manner in which these expenditures are financed. Governments do not as a rule determine their tax *revenues* directly: what they do is to set the *rates* of tax, which will yield different revenues depending upon future income and expenditure levels in the economy – levels which cannot of course be foreseen exactly when tax rates are set. Nor are governments always free to determine the amount of their foreign borrowing, although they may make decisions to seek more or less revenue of this kind. And since total expenditure must necessarily be matched by total revenue, a shortfall of one kind of revenue must be offset by an unanticipated increase in another. Usually, it is government borrowing from the domestic monetary system which serves as a residual source of finance.

Strictly, it might seem desirable to confine the term instrument to those things which governments actually determine directly – expenditure levels, tax rates and so on. The level of government borrowing would then be, not an instrument of fiscal policy, but instead the result of it. In practice however it is not possible to draw a line quite as simply as may be suggested by this brief discussion. Partly for this reason the term instrument will be used in this book in a rather looser sense, to include those things which government must reach decisions about, even though it does not control their levels directly. Hence, the levels of foreign borrowing and of borrowing from the monetary system are included among the instruments which are grouped together as aggregate fiscal policy.

1.42   *Aggregate Monetary Policy*

A practical definition of monetary policy raises similar, but in some respects even more difficult problems.

It is common for economists to explore the impact of monetary policy upon an economy by examining the effect in a short run macroeconomic model of a change in the stock of money. This tradition will be followed, to begin with at least, in the course of the next chapter. It is, however, a questionable one; for the stock of money (which is conventionally defined to include private sector bank deposits as well as the amount of cash held by members of the public) is rarely under the direct control of the monetary authority.

Now it might be suggested that a monetary authority must necessarily make decisions about the stock of money just as a fiscal authority must make decisions about the level of government borrowing, and that having extended the term instrument to include the latter, one must allow it to include the former as well. The two cases are not quite the same, however. Decisions about levels of borrowing are imposed upon governments by the logical necessity for income and expenditure accounts to balance. But no such accounting identity imposes decisions about the stock of money upon an economy's monetary authority. Indeed, to suppose that a monetary authority can in fact control the stock of money in an economy is to beg an important question, which will be examined in the next two chapters. If one wishes to leave this question open one cannot allow the term monetary policy to mean a change in the stock of money, nor can one use a change in the money stock as a measure of monetary policy. For the present, therefore, the term aggregate monetary policy will be used rather vaguely to refer to those things which central banks or other monetary authorities can do to influence the level of various monetary aggregates or the cost of money and credit.

This usage leads straight to a further major problem which is generally raised by an attempt to define monetary policy. Monetary aggregates and interest rates will be influenced in practice not only by what a monetary authority tries to do on its own initiative, but also by the amount and type of borrowing being undertaken by the fiscal authority. The latter have already been defined as instruments of fiscal policy, but one might equally well have chosen to define them as instruments of monetary policy. For the two are, quite clearly, very closely intertwined. It follows that an attempt to provide a practical but precise definition of monetary policy that is completely independent of a similar definition of fiscal policy would be a very difficult undertaking indeed.

This problem is important in other studies because the relative merits of fiscal and monetary policy have been a matter of considerable debate in economics in the last few decades. But it is not important in this book, because it is not concerned with that debate.

1.43   *Exchange Rate Policy*

In an open economy, the government – usually through its monetary authority – must decide whether to allow the value of its domestic currency in terms of those of other countries to be freely determined by market forces of one kind or another, or whether to fix it in terms of some standard. Most countries in the world chose the second alternative in the years between 1944 and 1972, and in this book it will be assumed unless otherwise stated that a fixed exchange rate system is in operation. A government which chooses such a system must make two further decisions, about the standard to which the domestic currency is to be related, and the fixed exchange rate between the domestic currency and that standard. These three decisions are the essence of exchange rate policy.

At any point in time, the result of these decisions is a set of exchange rates between the domestic currency of a single country, and the currencies of all other countries with which it engages in transactions. It is convenient to summarize this set of exchange rates in an appropriate index number, which is usually described as the 'effective exchange rate' of a particular domestic currency. In later chapters use will be made of such an index, representing the exchange rate between a country's currency and that of the 'average' foreign country with which it trades, as a measure of exchange rate policy.

It is important to note, once again, that this is to extend the term instrument to include something which government must necessarily make decisions about, even though in practice it cannot be controlled exactly. A currency's effective exchange rate often alters dramatically as a result of exchange rate decisions taken by other governments, as will be seen later in this book. When this happens, however, it seems reasonable to argue that a decision to take no action is as much a matter of policy as a decision to change the standard of the domestic currency, or to change the fixed exchange rate between the domestic currency and that standard. It is for this reason that the effective exchange rate is used here as a measure of exchange rate policy.

This has been a chapter of definitions – some of them precise, but many of them rather rough. Its purpose, like that of the chorus in a play, has been to introduce the important characters of the drama. As the drama unfolds these characters will gradually become more lifelike than they have been so far. But, since this is a book of economics, our next task is to disguise them beneath a layer of algebra.

NOTES

[1] In a discarded draft that was probably intended as a preface to *The General Theory of Employment, Interest and Money*.
[2] Sir A. Cairncross (ed.). *Britain's Economic Prospects Reconsidered* (Allen and Unwin, 1971), p. 168.
[3] J. M. Keynes, *The General Theory of Employment, Interest and Money* (Macmillan, 1936), p. 15.
[4] J. K. Galbraith, 'How Keynes Came to America', in *Economics, Peace and Laughter* (Penguin, 1975), p. 36.
[5] International Labour Office, *Employment, Incomes and Equality* (ILO, 1972).

SUGGESTED READING

D. Winch, *Economics and Policy: A Historical Study* (Fontana, 1972).
D. E. Moggridge, *Keynes* (Fontana, 1976).
Sir A. Cairncross, *Essays on Economic Management* (Allen and Unwin, 1971).

2 *Two Models of an Open Economy*

Economics is a science of thinking in terms of models ...

J. M. Keynes

2.1 INTRODUCTION

In the previous chapter it was argued that the essential meaning of stabilization policy is to be found in a theoretical tradition in economics – a tradition of using short run macroeconomic models to investigate the way in which some particular instruments and objectives of public policy are related in the real world. This tradition includes a large number of abstract models, two of which will be discussed in the present chapter.

They are both models of a small open economy, which may be defined here as one which is relatively unimportant in the foreign markets upon which it trades so that it can exert no influence upon the prices of its imports and exports, expressed in terms of foreign currency, by variations in the volumes which it buys and sells. Like the individual consumer or firm in perfect competition, the small open economy is a price taker. It may conveniently be thought of as producing two kinds of goods – exports (X), and goods destined for domestic markets (D); and as absorbing two kinds of goods – those produced domestically (D), and imports (M).

The two models are therefore of the same genus. But they are distinct species, and an important part of the purpose of this chapter is to emphasize the differences between them. This emphasis will not be entirely neutral, for an additional part of the chapter's purpose is to draw particular attention to the vices of one of the models (which is to be found in almost all contemporary textbooks of economics) and the virtues of the other (which in recent decades has not been found in textbooks at all). So the chapter contains an element of polemic, as well as exposition.

It also contains a number of footnotes, some of which are lengthy. Those footnotes, marked with an asterisk, contain explanations and qualifications which may be neglected by the reader who is interested merely in the broad structure of the argument, but which are nevertheless important for a full understanding of later chapters.

Finally, it contains a large number of symbols and a small amount of mathematics. The former (shown for easy reference in Table 2.1) provides an indispensable shorthand and requires no apology. The latter is occasionally necessary when the validity of particular points may not be obvious without proof. It is assumed only that the reader will be able to interpret (and, if he is of a suspicious mind, to check) the solution of a set of simultaneous equations. There are two first-order difference equations in the chapter as well, but the meaning of these will be roughly explained in the text, and the non-mathematical reader will then be able to see that he has been using first-order difference equations since he began to study economics, even though he may never have been asked to solve one explicitly.

TABLE 2.1
Symbols Used in Chapter 2 and Later Chapters

Flow Variables

A	domestic absorption
C	consumption expenditure
D	domestic expenditure on domestically produced goods and services
F	net foreign capital receipts
F_G	net foreign capital receipts of the public sector
F_P	net foreign capital receipts of the private sector (excluding banks)
G	government expenditure
I	investment expenditure (including stock changes)
I_I	intended investment expenditure (including stock changes)
I_U	unintended stock changes
M	imports of goods and services
X	exports of goods and services
Y	domestic output

Stock Variables

DA	domestic assets of the monetary system
DA_G	net lending by the monetary system to the public sector
DA_P	gross lending by the monetary system to the private sector
FR	foreign reserve assets of the monetary system
MO	the stock of money
PD	commercial bank deposits of the private sector

Index Numbers

P_A the price of domestic absorption, in units of domestic currency
P_M the price of imports, in units of foreign currency
P_X the price of exports, in units of foreign currency
P_Y the price of domestic output, in units of domestic currency
R the effective exchange rate between domestic and foreign currency

---

Miscellaneous Symbols

(i) Small letters (a, b, c, k, m, etc.) are used for parameters.

(ii) Square brackets [   ] are used to indicate a 'real' variable – that is, a nominal variable which has been deflated by an appropriate price index, as in the following example:

$$[Y] \equiv \frac{Y}{P_Y}.$$

(iii) A bar over a variable is used to indicate that it is assumed to be determined exogenously.

(iv) Subscripts (t, $t-1$, $t+1$, -1, $+1$, etc.) are used to indicate successive time periods. In general the t is suppressed. For a stock variable such as MO, the value of MO_t is taken to be its value at the end of period t.

(v) First differences are denoted by Δ. For example:

$$\Delta MO \equiv MO - MO_{-1}.$$

2.2   AN OUTPUT–DETERMINATION MODEL (ODM)

ODM 1: $[Y] \equiv [C] + [I] + [X] - [M]$.
ODM 2: $[C] = c[Y]$.
ODM 3: $[M] = m[Y]$.
ODM 4: $[X] = [\bar{X}]$.
ODM 5: $[I] = [\bar{I}_t]$.

When the reader has allowed his eye to become adjusted to the notation, he will recognize that the model presented in the form of equations ODM 1 to 5 is virtually identical to the simple model of an open economy that is to be found in most contemporary textbooks of macroeconomics, monetary theory and public finance. And it is not simply a textbook model. It provides a basic framework which in recent decades has been widely used by economists in governments and elsewhere for forecasting the behaviour of national economies, usually within a two or three year time horizon but sometimes for even longer periods.[1]

It is often referred to as a 'Keynesian' model. In one important respect this is an appropriate description, for the principal implication which is to be drawn from equations ODM 1 to 5 – namely, that economic activity will be at its full employment level only by accident or good management – is indeed the implication which Keynes drew from the model sketched in *The General Theory*. But in three other respects the description may be an unfair or unfortunate one. In the first place the equations contain no variables that are measured in terms of money, and no mention of money itself, whereas money was one of Keynes's major preoccupations. (This deficiency will be remedied shortly, in an informal manner.) Second, equations ODM 1 to 5 describe an open economy, whereas the model of *The General Theory* is one of a closed economy; and it will be suggested shortly that Keynes had good reason to restrict his focus in this way. And third, time is not mentioned explicitly in ODM, whereas there is a growing feeling amongst interpreters of Keynes that the model of *The General Theory* can only be understood properly if its time dimension is recognized. Again, more will be said about this point at a later stage in this chapter.

2.21   *The Meaning of the Equations*

ODM 1: $[Y] \equiv [C] + [I] + [X] - [M].$

This equation says that in any period of time domestic output $[Y]$ necessarily consists of goods and services which are consumed $[C]$, invested $[I]$ or exported $[X]$, less the imported component of these three kinds of expenditure – that is, total imports $[M]$. For the present it is convenient to treat this as a matter of definition, which may be modified as one wishes. For example it is useful for some purposes to distinguish as a separate category those goods and services which are absorbed by government $[G]$; in this chapter, however, it is assumed that these have been defined as part of $[I]$.

ODM 2: $[C] = c[Y].$

This is a highly simplified version of Keynes's 'fundamental psychological law' of consumption.[2] It says that the volume of consumption is a constant proportion[3*] of output.[4*] Any income which is not spent on consumption, according to this equation, may be thought of as going into savings, which may be taken for the present to include tax payments to the government.

ODM 3: $[M] = m[Y].$

This is the economy's import function, which says that imports are a constant proportion of output. It is less obvious than might at first appear that there should be a systematic relationship between these two variables, because an economy's imports are a part of its expenditures rather than its output. However, if imports are related in a simple linear manner to total expenditures in the economy including those made by foreigners, they will necessarily be related in a similar manner to the economy's output.[5*] So the equation may be interpreted as saying that imports are a constant proportion of $[C] + [I] + [X]$.

ODM 4: $[X] = [\bar{X}].$

This says that exports are assumed to be determined exogenously. The small open economy is of course able in principle to sell whatever it produces on world markets at the prices which prevail there. But in the short run with which this book is concerned, it may be assumed as a first approximation that the division of goods and services between domestic and export markets is fixed. (This first approximation will shortly be modified in an informal manner.)

ODM 5: $$[I] = [\bar{I}_t].$$

This equation says that actual investment is equal to intended investment, which is in turn determined exogenously by the decisions of government and the animal spirits of businessmen. In the present context, this equation is to be interpreted as an *equilibrium condition*.

2.22 *The Meaning of an Equilibrium Condition*

It is important to be precise about what an equilibrium condition means here. Equations ODM 1 to 5 are an attempt to describe in formal terms the structure of a *process* which takes place in the real world in a time dimension – a process in which consumers and firms make decisions about how much to consume, invest and import, and in which firms make decisions about how much to produce. But neither the time dimension nor firms' investment decisions appear explicitly in the equations.

In introductory expositions of the model these two missing elements are usually described in an informal manner, in terms of successive rounds of expenditure. There are many different ways in which this informal description can be given, but a typical example goes roughly as follows. Suppose that we begin with an economy in which all the equations are satisfied, but in which the typical firm is not producing as much with the resources available as it might; and that businessmen then suddenly become more optimistic about their future sales prospects, and start spending more on investment goods. In the first round, this higher level of *intended* investment will be met by a fall in stocks of investment goods which producing firms keep at hand to allow for fluctuations in sales. Since *actual* investment in the economy is defined to include changes in stocks, it will therefore be unaffected in this first round. But firms will then find that they have a lower level of stocks than they wish to hold, given their rate of sales. So in the next round they will increase *production* to make good the deficiency. This will mean higher incomes, and so higher consumption spending. In the second round higher consumption will be met by another unanticipated decline in stocks, which will mean an additional increase in production in the third round, and so on. The cumulative process will drive production in the economy to a new level, at which unintended changes in stocks are zero – that is, actual investment is equal to the new, higher level of intended investment.

The reader will recognize this informal description of the process that lies behind equation ODM 5 – or something very similar to the description, since textbooks are not uniform in this respect. It is a relatively straightforward matter to build such a description into the formal model by substituting two equations for ODM 5. The first of these defines actual investment as the sum of intended investment (which is still assumed to be determined exogenously) and unanticipated changes in stocks:

$$[I] = [\bar{I}_I] + [I_U].$$

And the second describes an adjustment process in which firms change their production levels in each time period to make good the unanticipated changes in stocks which took place in the previous period:

$$[Y]_{+1} = [Y] - [I_U].$$

(This equation, in which a time dimension is made explicit, is known as a first-order difference equation.)

One then has a set of six equations which describe fully an adjustment process for the whole economy, albeit a very simple one. They may be combined to yield the following first-order difference equation:

$$[Y]_{+1} - (c - m)[Y] = [\bar{I}_I] + [\bar{X}].$$

When one knows the value of $[Y]$ in one period and the values of the exogenous variables for all succeeding periods, one can use this equation to trace out the exact manner in which $[Y]$ will change in all future periods.

It is useful to have a general formula to describe this time path. As shown in any textbook of mathematics or mathematical economics which covers difference equations, the general solution of a first-order difference equation in the form

$$Y_{t+1} - bY_t = a$$

is as follows:

$$Y_t = \left(Y_0 - \frac{a}{1-b}\right)b^t + \frac{a}{1-b}.$$

The second expression on the right-hand side of the equation,

$$\frac{a}{1-b},$$

is a constant value towards which Y will move over time, if the absolute value of b is less than one; and the movement of Y towards this constant value will be steady rather than oscillatory if b is positive.

The solution of our particular first-order difference equation is thus:

$$[Y]_t = \left([Y]_0 - \frac{[\bar{I}_I] + [\bar{X}]}{1 - c + m}\right) \cdot (c - m)^t + \frac{[\bar{I}_I] + [\bar{X}]}{1 - c + m}.$$

If the value of $(c - m)$ is positive but less than one, output will move towards a constant value at which it may easily be shown that unanticipated changes in stocks are zero.

Equation ODM 5 may therefore be interpreted as saying that the economy has reached a stable, 'equilibrium' position towards which an adjustment process is assumed to be driving it. This adjustment process is not made explicit in equations ODM 1 to 5, but nevertheless it underlies model ODM as a representation of the way a real-world economy behaves.

Some time has been spent on this point for two main reasons. First, the use of an equilibrium condition such as ODM 5 rather than a fully specified adjustment process disguises a problem in the empirical application of model ODM, which will be touched upon later in this book. Second, it tends to make ODM seem simpler than it really is, particularly when this model is contrasted with others in which an adjustment process is more fully specified (such as the second model presented in this chapter). However, when its nature is understood, an equilibrium condition is an extremely useful simplifying device and it will be used regularly in this chapter.

2.23 *Implications of the Model*

(i) *Economic activity.* The first implication of ODM is that there is an equilibrium level of output in the economy, determined by the parameters of the model and by the values of its exogenously determined variables. By combining equations ODM 1 to 5 one may obtain the following expression for this equilibrium output:

$$[Y] = \frac{[X] + [I_l]}{1 - c + m}.$$

(This is, of course, exactly the same as the constant value towards which $[Y]$ was seen to be tending in our difference equation.)

Equilibrium output is thus the product of what is usually described as 'autonomous expenditure' $[X] + [I_l]$, and the 'multiplier',

$$\frac{1}{1 - c + m}.$$

The economy's potential output at full employment does not enter into this expression. According to ODM, it will therefore happen only by accident or good management that full employment output will be achieved.

An obvious problem arises at this point: what happens to an economy in practice if its full employment output should be *below* ODM's equilibrium level? Clearly, ODM's equations cannot be satisfied in this situation. It is commonly described in textbooks as an 'inflationary gap', indicating a belief that the result of such a contradiction will be a tendency for prices to rise. But a model in which all variables are *real* variables and in which no time dimension is included cannot, by its very nature, provide an explanation of an inflationary process. To explain inflation ODM must first be extended, as will be seen in a moment.

(ii) *The balance of payments.* So far ODM contains no implications about the behaviour of the balance of payments, in the strict sense of that term. But one important part of the record of a country's international transactions, namely the balance on current account, may be derived from it quite simply. For ODM assumes a level of exports and implies an equilibrium level of imports, both expressed in real terms; the assumption of a small open economy allows one to multiply these levels by exogenously determined export and import prices (P_X and P_M) to derive the current account balance expressed in terms of foreign currency; to convert this into a balance expressed in terms of domestic currency it is simply necessary to deflate it by the effective exchange rate, which is by assumption a variable determined by government policy. The equilibrium current account balance is therefore

$$\frac{[\bar{X}] \cdot \bar{P}_X - [M] \cdot \bar{P}_M}{\bar{R}}.$$

To proceed from this expression to an equation for the equilibrium level of the economy's balance of payments in our strict sense, ΔFR, all that is then required is to take the capital account balance F as given exogenously (or, what amounts to the same thing, as depending upon variables such as the level of domestic interest rates which will not be incorporated here into the formal model). One can thus add a further equation to ODM:

ODM 6: $$\Delta FR = \frac{[\bar{X}] \cdot \bar{P}_X}{\bar{R}} - \frac{[M] \cdot \bar{P}_M}{\bar{R}} + \bar{F}.$$

This equation is a reasonable representation of the way in which most economic forecasters proceed when predicting balance of payments developments.[6*] The important point to notice about it is that although developments in the domestic economy have an effect upon the balance of payments through their effect upon [M], there is nothing self-regulating about ODM's balance of payments. Like full employment output, payments balance will only be achieved by accident or good management. And in ODM 'good management' may well be an ambiguous concept: for there is no reason why particular targets for its level of economic activity and balance of payments should be consistent with one another.

(iii) *Prices*. The appearance of import prices and the effective exchange rate in ODM's equations is a useful step towards a theory of prices, since imports are one of the two general kinds of goods and services which should appear in an appropriate index of the domestic price level. But the equations which have been presented so far contain no implications about the price of the other kind, namely those that are produced domestically [D]. However they can be made to do so by extending ODM, in the spirit of *The General Theory*, along the following lines.

If competition obliges employers to hire labour at a point where its marginal product is equal to its real wage rate, an equilibrium level of output implies an equilibrium real wage rate – at least in the short run, when the economy's capital stock is determined exogenously. But the real wage rate is simply the nominal wage rate deflated by the price of output. So if one can provide an additional equation in the model to explain the behaviour of the nominal wage rate, the price of domestic output will be fully determined.

There has been a great deal of controversy about how this step should be taken. Some economists have been content simply to assume an exogenous nominal wage rate, fixed by institutional or psychological factors. Inflation is then seen as a phenomenon to be explained by political scientists or social psychologists, rather than economists. Others have sought to bring nominal wage *changes* into the system of equations endogenously, linking them to the gap between output and its full employment level by means of a relationship known as the Phillips curve. (This curve was first presented in 1958 as an empirical generalization about the behaviour of nominal wages in the UK, but it has subsequently acquired an international following and a variety of theoretical explanations – which have inevitably become more complex, as the original generalization by Phillips has broken down in practice.) The addition of something like the Phillips curve can therefore provide ODM with an ability to account for *inflation*, although not, of course, the absolute *level* of prices.

In practice the distinction between these two groups of economists is an important one, because different beliefs about the determinants of nominal wage changes in the real world lead the two groups to very different views about what governments can do to control rates of domestic inflation. But their theories of inflation have the common feature that they may be set down formally in systems of equations in which the stock of money in the economy does not appear as a variable. For the stock of money has yet to make an appearance in this discussion. It is time for this omission to be rectified, if only because Keynes devoted a great deal of attention to money in *The General Theory*.

2.24 *The Role of Money in the Output-determination Model*

To begin with, we shall make the conventional assumption that the nominal stock of money in circulation, MO, is determined exogenously by the government through its monetary authority:

$$MO = \check{M}O.$$

This money stock must be held by the public. So the question is raised: what determines the amount of money which will be held willingly by the economy's firms and households?

The Cambridge tradition in which Keynes was brought up, and to which he contributed in the 1920s in his *Tract on Monetary Reform* and *Treatise on Money*, provided a reasonably straightforward answer to this question. Put simply, it was that the demand for nominal money balances in an economy depends upon the level of nominal income and output:

$$MO = k \cdot Y.$$

It was recognized that k could vary, in the short run in response to changes in interest rates or expectations about future inflation, and in the long run in response to institutional changes. In formal theorizing, however, the Cambridge tradition before *The General Theory* tended to regard k as an approximate constant.

It was however crucial to the argument of *The General Theory* that k should *not* be constant. For the two equations that have appeared in this section would then determine a unique level of nominal output. Keynes already had a theory of economic activity; and, as was suggested in the previous section, he already had a rough theory of the price of output. So a further theory of nominal output was not only unnecessary for him – it would also create an inconsistency.

Hence Keynes's insistence in his discussion of 'liquidity preference' in *The General Theory*, that k varies with the level of interest rates (or more erratically perhaps, with the climate of business opinion concerning the future course of interest rates). The level of interest rates, in turn, was given an important role in *The General Theory* as an influence on the level of intended investment.

This brief outline of Keynes's approach explains the way in which ODM is extended in textbooks to include a monetary system.[7]* Confronted by a fixed stock of money, the demand for money balances determines the level of interest rates; the level of interest rates in turn affects $[I_I]$, which then becomes an endogenously determined variable. But the monetary system's behaviour is not allowed to affect anything else directly in extended versions of ODM.

And even this modest function has seemed to some of Keynes's successors (most especially perhaps, in Britain in the 1950s and early 1960s) to be one which might safely be neglected in practice. The neglect could be justified by any of three distinct arguments. In the first place, it might be the case that firms' investment plans depend hardly at all upon the level of interest rates, so that money and interest cease to have an important influence upon the behaviour of any *real* variables in the model. Second, it might be the case that very large changes in k can be brought about by minimal changes in the rate of interest, so that firms and households can be persuaded to hold whatever amount of money the authorities choose to supply without anything else being affected – a situation which has come to be described as a 'liquidity trap'. These first two arguments are essentially about the value of particular parameters in extended versions of ODM. They can be settled, in principle, by empirical investigation of the interest-elasticity of firms' intended investment and of k.

Third, it might be the case that the stock of money is not under the control of the authorities at all, but instead is an irrelevant variable which adjusts itself automatically so as to match whatever need the community feels for it. When discussed in contemporary textbooks this third argument is generally treated as a rather extreme one; but like most 'extreme' ideas in economics it has a long history. And it has an important place in modern economics too. For in practice the extensions to ODM which have been sketched in this section have not, at least until very recently, had a great deal of influence upon the formal models with which most contemporary economic forecasters attempt to predict the behaviour of economies in the real world.

2.25 *Equilibrium Output and Full Employment*

The radical conclusion of *The General Theory* which is reproduced by ODM was that any economy's output could be in 'equilibrium' below its full employment level. The instinctive response of Keynes's predecessors, which he attempted to counter in advance, might have been on something like the following lines: with output below its full employment level, some workers will be seeking jobs at nominal wages lower than those that currently prevail, and firms will simultaneously have an incentive to cut their prices – at least upon domestic markets, where each one could hope to sell more by doing so; the level of nominal wages and prices will therefore tend to fall, and this will restore the economy to full employment. Unlike many of his successors, Keynes was not content with a simple denial that typical firms and workers in a modern economy act in this way. Instead he insisted that even if they do so, full employment may not be restored. But his argument succeeds only in very special circumstances.

A convenient place to begin an examination of this argument is ODM's expression for the equilibrium level of output:

$$\frac{[I_I] + [X]}{1 - c + m}.$$

According to this expression, a fall in the level of domestic prices will tend to raise $[Y]$ towards its full employment level only to the extent that it raises $[X]$, $[I_I]$ or c, or lowers m. There are of course many ways in which these exogenous variables and parameters of ODM might be affected. Here we shall discuss only three, starting with what is probably in practice the least important.

This first possibility was considered by Keynes at some length. As domestic prices fall, the real value of an exogenously determined nominal stock of money will tend to rise. In order for this increased *real* stock of money to be held willingly, interest rates would have to fall. This should tend, in turn, to raise $[I_I]$ and hence the equilibrium level of $[Y]$. However, two possible obstacles upon this route to full employment have already been noted: the increase in $[Y]$ may be halted if the interest-elasticity of $[I_I]$ becomes zero, or if that of k becomes infinite. The route may thus seem uncertain, and perhaps also unnecessarily lengthy and painful.

The second possibility is one which Keynes neglected.[8*] As prices fall and the real value of money rises, holders of existing money balances will be better off. Even if their real income remains constant, they may be expected to consume some part of this increase in their wealth. So the coefficient c will rise. And this rise in c and hence in $[Y]$ will continue until prices are stable once again – that is to say, according to the hypothesis with which this section began, until full employment is reached.

This mechanism is known variously as the 'real balance effect', 'wealth effect' or 'Pigou effect'. It has had a somewhat chequered career in economic literature. Its theoretical foundations were hotly contested in the 1940s and 1950s, precisely because its implications are so damaging to the possibility of an 'unemployment equilibrium' which Keynes claimed to have established in *The General Theory*. The theoretical contest was settled in favour of the validity of the real balance mechanism, as conclusively as is possible in these matters, by the end of the 1950s. And interpreters of *The General Theory* were then faced with two alternative possibilities – to concede that Keynes's argument was wrong, and that an unemployment equilibrium could only exist if prices and wages were in practice inflexible downwards; or to reinterpret Keynes as having argued, not that an unemployment *equilibrium* was possible, but rather that the dynamics of the adjustment process might be such that the only possible equilibrium level of output, its full employment level, would never be reached.[9]* On the whole most economic theorists chose the first alternative, until the publication of Leijonhufvud's major study *On Keynesian Economics and the Economics of Keynes* in 1968 made the second a respectable view to hold.

But neither the technical knockout which was scored by the real balance effect, nor Leijonhufvud's reinterpretation of *The General Theory*, have been allowed to disturb the dominance of ODM and its 'unemployment equilibrium' in economics textbooks. In the first case, the response of the textbooks was to cast doubt upon the practical significance of the real balance mechanism. Thus one writer, after an extremely lucid summary of the mechanism, commented as follows upon the possibility that it could work in such a way as to stabilize output at its full employment level:

> I do not believe this. The Pigou effect ... stresses a relation that may exist, but normally as a very minor factor.[10]

And in the 1960s and early 1970s economists who were engaged in practical macroeconomic forecasting remained similarly unaffected by the theoretical controversy over the real balance effect. The consumption functions which they employed almost always related consumption to income, and nothing else.

And so things might have continued, but for the world-wide inflation of the early 1970s. But as prices accelerated upwards, economic forecasters who based their projections upon a model similar to ODM discovered, with remarkable unanimity, that their forecasts of consumption were too high. This experience has led to a reappraisal of the main forecasting models, and of their consumption functions in particular. It is of course much too early to be sure why the problem arose; but work published by the Bank of England in 1976, in its *Quarterly Bulletin*, suggests very strongly that the error arose in Britain precisely because an important real balance mechanism was missing from the consumption functions used by economic forecasters. The real balance mechanism may well turn out to deserve more than a footnote in the textbooks.

The third and perhaps the most important route to full employment when prices are flexible downwards is one that Keynes conceded, without a struggle, in a few sentences of *The General Theory*.[11] In an open economy with a fixed exchange rate, a fall in domestic prices will induce firms to switch resources to the production of exports, to the extent that possibilities exist for such substitution. Similarly, domestic firms and households will tend to switch their purchases from imports to domestic production.[12]* There will therefore be some tendency for [X] to rise, and for the coefficient m to fall; and the equilibrium level of [Y] will tend to rise towards its full employment level. This point was so obvious to Keynes that it required no elaboration.

It follows from these arguments that if ODM's 'equilibrium' level of output below full employment is really to be a constant value towards which Y will tend, firms must be assumed *not* to respond in this situation by adjusting their prices downwards. When they find that they are producing more than they can sell at the prevailing price level, their response is to cut production rather than to cut prices. Now it may well be that this is how most large firms, particularly in industrialized economies, do actually tend to behave. But model ODM will be strictly valid only if *all* firms behave in this way, all the time. There is then no room in ODM for a theory of the domestic price level: it must be determined exogenously by past history. And if this is so, one does not require ODM's consumption function and multiplier to demonstrate that output [Y] may settle below its full employment level. All that is required for this purpose is a theory to explain the level of nominal income, Y.

2.26 *Conclusions*

The preceding discussion has been designed to highlight two principal problems with ODM. The first of these is that its essential implications are confined to the behaviour of output. Only by grafting extra bits and pieces onto it in a rather *ad hoc* way can it be made to yield implications about the behaviour of the balance of payments and the rate of inflation, and in the latter case the graft is difficult to make in a satisfactory manner. And the second problem is that ODM's equilibrium level of output turns out, on close examination, to be an equilibrium only in very special circumstances, and perhaps to be something quite different from what Keynes was talking about in *The General Theory*. For many years the student who pursues macroeconomic theory in any depth has found that he has had to abandon ODM's straightforward implication of an equilibrium level of output, and its simple multiplier.

These are serious aesthetic weaknesses for a textbook model. But they do not necessarily amount to a criticism of ODM as a simple means of providing the student with a greater understanding of the world in which he lives, as a basis for forecasting the behaviour of national economies, or as a practical guide that may be relied upon in the conduct of stabilization policy. The issue here is not aesthetic, but empirical. It hinges upon whether stable parameters for behavioural equations such as ODM's consumption and import functions can be identified from past experience, and used with confidence for future prediction of the behaviour of a national economy's output. It hinges, in short, upon whether a stable multiplier exists.

2.3 A MODEL OF FINANCIAL FLOWS (MFF)

MFF 1:	$Y = A + \bar{X} - M.$
MFF 2:	$MO = kY.$
MFF 3:	$M = mY.$
MFF 4:	$\Delta MO = \Delta FR + \Delta \bar{D}A.$
MFF 5:	$\Delta FR = \bar{X} - M + \bar{F}.$

Our second model, which is summarized in equations MFF 1 to 5, is not similar to anything that is to be found in the standard economics textbooks of the last few decades. Its origins, however, lie much further back in history than those of ODM. Something very similar to it was sketched in 1720 by an economist called Isaac Gervaise,[13] and its implications have been familiar to practical bankers and financiers for more than two centuries. But it was not until 1957 that a formal account of this model and its implications was developed by J. J. Polak in the International Monetary Fund,[14] and it was not until the 1960s that academic economists began to show a serious interest once again in models similar to MFF (which is a special case of what is now known as the monetary theory of the balance of payments).[15] So MFF's structure and implications are still unfamiliar to many economists.

2.31 *The Meaning of the Equations*

MFF 1: $Y = A + \bar{X} - M.$

This is the national accounting identity that has already appeared in this book as equation ODM 1, apart from three obvious modifications. First, all its variables are now defined in nominal rather than real terms. Second, the distinction between consumption and investment expenditures has now been dropped; the two are lumped together as domestic absorption, A. And third, the assumption that exports are treated as being exogenously determined has been incorporated in the equation, to save space. (This is why it is now written as an equation, not an identity.)

MFF 2: $MO = kY.$

This equation has already been encountered in Section 2.24, as the Cambridge approach to the demand for money. In what follows k will be treated as a constant. (There is no great difficulty in principle about allowing k to be a variable in MFF, determined by other variables such as the level of interest rates and the rate of inflation; but if this is done the model's implications will of course become rather more complex than those that will be described.)

MFF 3: $M = mY.$

This import function is almost identical to equation ODM 3. But the relationship is now one between nominal rather than real variables, and this represents an important change of meaning. For MFF 3 implies that when other things remain equal a given increase in the price of imports, in terms of domestic currency, will lead to an exactly equal relative decline in import volume. The reader may wish to interpret this as an assumption that the price-elasticity of demand for imports is unity, but he will not be encouraged here to use this terminology.[16]*

At this point in the examination of MFF's equations it is convenient to pause for reflection. In equations MFF 1 to 3 there are five variables (Y, A, $\bar{X}$, M and MO), one of which has been assumed to be determined exogenously. If we were now to assume that MO is determined exogenously by the monetary authority, as we did throughout the earlier discussion of ODM, there would be three independent equations containing only three unknowns. The system would be determinate.

But it is time to abandon the assumption that the central bank of a small open economy can directly control the stock of money in domestic circulation. For in an open economy, MO changes not only when it is increased or withdrawn from circulation by the central bank and the commercial banks under its supervision. It also changes over time as domestic money stocks are reduced or augmented by flows of money across the foreign exchanges. These flows are a reflection of decisions taken by foreign and domestic residents about our economy's imports and exports – decisions about which assumptions have already been made in MFF 1 and MFF 3. So the central bank is only able to control the amount of money in domestic circulation to the extent that it is able to 'sterilize' these flows, by exactly compensating variations in the amount of money that is put into circulation or withdrawn from it by the domestic monetary system. In an open economy it therefore seems appropriate to regard *this* variable, which is known to economists as 'domestic credit expansion' or DCE for short, as the exogenous monetary aggregate in the model. For the influence of the monetary authority over DCE is direct, whereas the behaviour of the money stock reflects, in addition, the decisions of domestic and foreign residents and firms about which explicit assumptions have already been made.

Since the concepts of domestic credit and DCE often seem somewhat mysterious when they are first encountered, and since this may be the first occasion on which the reader has encountered them, a concrete illustration of their meaning may be useful at this point. This illustration is based upon the balance sheets of the Central Bank and commercial banks of Kenya at the end of 1973. These balance sheets are shown in Table 2.2, very roughly in the form in which they appear in official statistical publications, together with a consolidation.

There are of course an infinite variety of ways in which a balance sheet may be consolidated. The particular consolidation which is shown in Table 2.2 has been chosen to illustrate the concepts of domestic credit and DCE in a practical context. It has been arrived at by two steps. First, one groups together on the left-hand side of the consolidated balance sheet, as liabilities of the monetary system, those items which are conventionally defined as money,[17]* and one groups all other items together as assets on the right-hand side. In the process, any item which originally appeared as an asset of the Central Bank and a liability of the commercial banks, or the other way round, disappears from view.

TABLE 2.2
Assets and Liabilities of the Monetary System in Kenya at the End of 1973

Millions of Kenya Shillings (K.sh.)

Item	Central Bank Liabilities		Item	Central Bank Assets	
1	Currency held by public	982	6	Foreign Exchange	1477
2	Currency held by Com. Banks	137	7	Kenya Govt. Securities	176
3	Deposits of Kenya Govt.	330	8	Direct advances to Kenya Govt.	200
4	Deposits of Com. Banks	234	9	Other (net)	(159)
5	Deposits of External Banks	11			

Item	Commercial Bank Liabilities		Item	Commercial Bank Assets	
10	Private Sector Deposits	3836	14	Cash	137
11	Public Sector Deposits	723	15	Balances at Central Bank	234
12	Balances due to External Banks	109	16	Balances due by External Banks	96
			17	Kenya Govt. Treasury Bills	460
			18	Investments*	455
13	Other (Net)	(58)	19	Advances to Public Sector	224
			20	Advances to Private Sector	3004

CONSOLIDATION

Liabilities of the Monetary System		Assets of the Monetary System	
MO: Money Stock (Items 1 + 10)	4818	FR: Foreign Assets $(6 - 5 - 12 + 16)$	1453
		DA: Domestic Assets:	
Other (Net): $(13 - 9)$	101	$DA_G(7 + 8 - 3 - 11 + 17 + 18 + 19)$	462
		DA_P (20)	3004

Source: Central Bank of Kenya, *Annual Report 1974.*
* In Kenya, this item consists almost entirely of short term lending to a government institution, the Cereals and Sugar Finance Corporation.

Second, the assets which remain on the right-hand side after this process are divided into the two broad categories, foreign assets (FR), and domestic assets (DA), in accordance with a balance sheet identity:

$$MO \equiv FR + DA.$$

Now it may be seen from Table 2.2 that in the Kenyan context, almost all of the items which remain on the right-hand side after the first step (apart from a small residual, which may be neglected in empirical work provided that it remains roughly constant over time) may be assigned unambiguously to one or other of the following three groups:

(i) net foreign assets;
(ii) net indebtedness of the Kenya Government and other public sector bodies to the Central Bank and commercial banks; and
(iii) commercial bank loans and advances to the private sector.

Thus the phrase 'the domestic assets of the monetary system', or 'domestic credit', for short, can be given a precise practical meaning as the total of groups (ii) and (iii) in this list.

Furthermore this total is an important one in the analysis of policy. For *changes* in government net indebtedness to the monetary system were explicitly defined in Chapter 1 as an instrument of fiscal policy. And the level of commercial bank lending to the private sector is an aggregate which every central bank in a mixed economy attempts from time to time to influence or control. There is therefore nothing in the least mysterious about the concept of domestic credit, or the change in this total from one period of time to the next – namely, DCE.[18*]

This concludes our digression: we can now proceed to the remaining two equations of MFF.

MFF 4: $\Delta MO = \Delta FR + \Delta \bar{D}A.$

This equation is simply our balance sheet formula for an economy's monetary system, transformed for convenience into first difference form, and with DCE introduced as an exogenous variable reflecting the budgetary decisions of the government, and the monetary authority's control over commercial bank lending to the private sector.

MFF 5: $\Delta FR = \bar{X} - M + \bar{F}.$

This final equation is the balance of payments identity, with exports and the capital account balance F treated for present purposes as exogenously determined variables.

In these last two equations, a time dimension has been introduced explicitly into MFF. And an adjustment process has implicitly been introduced as well. But since this adjustment process is not altogether obvious from the equations, it may be useful if an informal sketch is provided at this point.

The clue to an understanding of the adjustment mechanism implicit in MFF 1 to 5 is the fact that MO appears in the model both as a *stock* at different points in time, and as a *flow* in each period of time. The latter role may be seen most clearly, perhaps, if the identities upon which equations MFF 4 and MFF 5 are based are combined with the definition of ΔMO to yield the following expression:

$$MO \equiv MO_{-1} + X + F + \Delta DA - M.$$

This expression may be paraphrased as follows: the stock of money in domestic circulation at the end of each period will necessarily be equal to what it was at the beginning, plus what has been injected into the domestic circulation by foreigners and the domestic monetary system, less whatever has leaked out to pay for imports. But when extra money is injected into the circulation by F or ΔDA, there will not be a *simultaneous* increase in the amount which domestic residents are willing to hold. For the demand for money is determined, according to equation MFF 2, by income Y (which is the sum of exports X, and income from domestic sales of domestically produced goods D). So in the first instance the extra money must be passed on as additional expenditure. But this additional spending must be spending either on imports M, or on domestically produced goods D. It will therefore have two effects upon MO: first, by raising D and hence Y, it will increase the amount of MO which residents are willing to hold; and second, by raising M it will reduce the amount of MO which is actually in circulation. So equation MFF 2, which says that k is constant in each time period, will be satisfied at a new level of both MO and Y. But in the next time period, since MO_{-1} will be different, the adjustment process must be repeated.

This description can be condensed in a variety of ways. For example, one might say that variations in the rate of monetary expenditure act as an equilibrating force bringing the demand for and supply of money in the economy into equality. Or one might say that the stock of money adjusts passively to whatever level is necessary, given the level of monetary expenditure and hence of nominal income. These are alternative descriptions of the same process: they are not alternative interpretations of MFF.

2.32   *Implications for Nominal Income and the Balance of Payments*

(i) *Nominal income.* MFF provides, first of all, a simple theory of the level of nominal income. Equations MFF 2 to 5 may be combined straightforwardly into the following first-order difference equation:

$$Y - \left(\frac{k}{k+m}\right) \cdot Y_{-1} = \frac{\bar{X} + \bar{F} + \Delta \bar{D}A}{k+m}.$$

This equation has the solution:

$$Y_t = \left(Y_0 - \frac{\bar{X} + \bar{F} + \Delta \bar{D}A}{m}\right) \cdot \left(\frac{k}{k+m}\right)^t + \frac{\bar{X} + \bar{F} + \Delta \bar{D}A}{m}.$$

As was seen in Section 2.22, what this solution says is that Y will move from wherever it starts towards a constant value, namely

$$\frac{\bar{X} + \bar{F} + \Delta \bar{D}A}{m}$$

and it will do so in a stable manner.[19*] A concrete example may be useful here. Suppose that the chosen time period is one-quarter of a year; that the value of m is 0.5 and the value of k is 1.5 (very roughly corresponding to the actual figures in Kenya in the late 1960s); that the initial values of all variables in period 0 are zero; and that from period 1 onwards the value of the exogenous variables $X + F + \Delta DA$ is constant at 50. The constant towards which Y will move is then 100; and according to the above solution, the values which Y will take in each period 1 onwards will be as follows:

$$25, \; 43.8, \; 57.8, \; 68.4, \; 76.3, \; 82.2, \; 86.7, \; 90.0, \ldots$$

Thus 90 per cent of the adjustment will be complete within two years.

So nominal income has an equilibrium value in MFF, depending solely upon the three exogenous variables and the coefficient m. It may seem surprising at first glance that this equilibrium level of Y is completely independent of the coefficient k, but a simple informal explanation can be provided. As Y moves towards its equilibrium value, all the other endogenous variables must move towards equilibrium values as well, since they are linked to Y by MFF's equations. So if Y reaches its equilibrium value, MO does so simultaneously: there is no tendency for holders of money balances to change the amount in circulation. In equilibrium there is therefore only one leakage from the monetary circulation – the leakage through imports. So it is the size of this leakage which determines, together with the value of autonomous injections into the monetary circulation, the equilibrium level of nominal income.

(ii) *The balance of payments.* Economists were first led to a formal examination of models such as MFF by an interest in the behaviour of the balance of payments. MFF's implications about this variable are both simple and powerful. The reader who is not familiar with these implications must be warned, however, that he should prepare for some surprises.

A convenient starting point is provided by equation MFF 4. As has been shown, this equation is based upon a balance sheet identity which is by itself of no theoretical significance:

$$\Delta FR \equiv \Delta MO - \Delta DA.$$

This identity acquires theoretical significance in MFF because ΔDA is treated as an exogenously determined variable, and because ΔMO is an endogenous variable which tends towards zero as the model moves to its equilibrium. So in equilibrium, the balance of payments is determined by ΔDA and nothing else.

According to MFF, therefore, those governments which attempt to cure a balance of payments deficit by stimulating exports, by encouraging the inflow of capital or discouraging its outflow, and by encouraging import-substituting industries or restricting imports, seem doomed to failure. These measures may well affect other variables of the model, but they will do nothing whatever to the equilibrium of the balance of payments except to the extent that ΔDA is *also* restricted. And if ΔDA *is* restricted, the effect of this upon the equilibrium of the balance of payments will not depend at all upon whether other measures are put into effect. They are irrelevant.

Now this conclusion may well seem rather strange, and perhaps even rather perverse. For if the relationship between the balance of payments and fiscal and monetary policies affecting ΔDA is indeed so straightforward, why has it not been obvious to many governments (and economists) during the last few decades?

Model MFF itself provides a simple explanation. In any period of time its endogenous variables are likely to be moving towards their equilibrium values. So MO will be *changing*, and this will prevent a domestic credit expansion from having an immediate mirror-image in a balance of payments deficit. The simple relationship between ΔDA and ΔFR will hold in equilibrium, but in the real world equilibrium may never be reached. The simple relationship can then easily cease to be obvious.

When the possibility of disequilibrium is admitted, the behaviour of exports and capital flows will affect the balance of payments in MFF. An increase in $X + F$, for example, will raise the equilibrium level of Y, and therefore MO; if ΔDA remains constant, ΔFR must then improve for as long as MO is in the process of adjustment to its higher equilibrium. More generally, therefore, MFF implies that the behaviour of the balance of payments ΔFR over time will be determined in a rather complex manner by:

  (i) the level of ΔDA; and
  (ii) *changes* in the level of $X + F$.

It is important to note the element of asymmetry between these two influences. The first is a change in a *stock* variable, between the end of one period and the next; the second is a change in the rate of a *flow* between two periods.

2.33   *Implications for Prices and Economic Activity*

So far MFF has been examined as an adjustment process. From now on, however, we shall concentrate for simplicity upon its implications when Y is at its equilibrium level:

$$\frac{X + F + \Delta DA}{m}.$$

This equilibrium level implies, at any given level of domestic output $[Y]$, a single price level for this output P_Y. Alternatively, at any given level of P_Y, it implies a single level of $[Y]$. So if assumptions are made about either one of these variables, MFF's explanation of the level of nominal income Y provides a theory to explain the other. (Ideally, of course, one would like to have a theory to explain how a change in nominal income will split into its price and output components in a time dimension. But this is a matter to which monetary economists have only recently begun to turn their attention; so for the present we shall make do with simple assumptions about the behaviour of output or prices in equilibrium.)

Before proceeding, the reader should remind himself of the argument which was presented in Section 2.25, whose conclusions may be summarized as follows:

  (i) if prices respond in both directions to excess demands and supplies of commodities and factors of production, the only possible equilibrium level of output is a full employment level;
  (ii) it is possible that the precise mechanics of the adjustment process may be such that this equilibrium will not be reached, as Leijonhufvud has suggested that Keynes was arguing in *The General Theory*; and
  (iii) if prices do not respond downwards in the face of excess supplies of commodities and factors of production, there can be an equilibrium level of output below full employment.

In what follows it will be assumed that prices are flexible, and that the full employment level of output can be reached; and we shall investigate the behaviour of prices on these assumptions. In order to avoid begging unnecessary questions, however, we shall speak of an 'equilibrium' level of prices.

The obvious first step, then, is to add to MFF an expression for the equilibrium level of output:

MFF 6: $[Y] = [\bar{Y}]$.

This is an equilibrium in the same sense as the equilibrium level of Y which has already been derived: that is, it is a constant value towards which $[Y]$ will tend, on particular assumptions. But it is perhaps important to note that there is no reason to expect the economy to move towards these two equilibria at the same rate. This is a practical problem which the use of an equilibrium condition in equation MFF 6 rather than a fully specified adjustment process allows one to neglect.

Equations MFF 1 to 6 may not be combined straightforwardly to yield an expression for the equilibrium level of P_y :

$$P_y = \frac{\bar{X} + \bar{F} + \Delta \bar{D} \bar{A}}{m \cdot [Y]}.$$

P_y is however an index of prices in transactions where domestic residents act as *sellers* rather than *buyers*. It is therefore not quite the same as the concept of a general price level which was defined in Section 1.22 as a concern of stabilization policy. What is wanted instead is a measure of the price of domestic absorption A, which may be defined as follows:

MFF 7: $$P_A \equiv \frac{A}{[A]} \equiv \frac{A}{[D] + [M]} \equiv \frac{A}{[Y] - [X] + [M]}.$$

To see how the equilibrium value of P_A is determined, it is necessary to add two further equations (which appeared implicitly in model ODM, in Section 2.23):

MFF 8: $$X = \frac{[\check{X}] . \bar{P}_X}{\bar{R}},^{20*} \text{ and}$$

MFF 9: $$M = \frac{[M] . \bar{P}_M}{\bar{R}}.$$

Model MFF now has all the equations that are needed to determine an equilibrium domestic price level. But the expression for the equilibrium level of P_A which results from the combination of these equations is unfortunately a rather cumbersome one,[21*] and for present purposes it is useful to reduce it to reasonable proportions by introducing two simplifying assumptions – first, that F and ΔDA are both zero; and second, that P_X and P_M are both equal to a single 'foreign' price level, which will be denoted by P_X alone. These assumptions allow one to derive a simple expression for the equilibrium level of P_A from model MFF, as follows:

$$P_A = \frac{\bar{P}_X . [\check{X}]}{\bar{R} . m . [\bar{Y}]}.$$

The important implications of this equation are that the equilibrium domestic price level P_A will depend positively upon the foreign price level P_X, and inversely upon the effective exchange rate R, in a very simple manner: a one per cent rise in P_X will lead to a one per cent rise in P_A; and so too will a one per cent fall in (or depreciation of) the effective exchange rate R.

Now, a relaxation of the restrictive assumptions upon which this result is based will of course mean that they will have to be modified somewhat. But in practice, in any economy in which imports and exports amount separately to a quarter or more of domestic income, the modifications which are necessary usually turn out to be surprisingly small. The important implications of MFF about the equilibrium level of P_A are, therefore, its *positive* dependence upon prices upon world markets, and its *inverse* dependence upon the effective exchange rate.

There is one final note to be added to this section. The discussion so far has been based upon the assumption that the exchange rate is fixed exogenously by the authorities: it is not one of the prices which adjusts in response to excess demands and supplies. If this assumption is abandoned, MFF's implications become rather different.

The most obvious alternative is to assume a perfectly flexible exchange rate, which may be defined as one which will vary in such a way as to ensure that the domestic demand for foreign currency (M) is always exactly equal to the supply $(X + F)$.[22*] This means that ΔFR will be zero in every time period. According to equation MFF 4, changes in domestic credit will then be the *sole* determinant of changes in *MO*; according to MFF 2, they will thus be the *sole* determinant of changes in Y; and according to MFF 6, they will thus be the *sole* determinant of changes in the equilibrium of P_Y. Almost every variable including the effective exchange rate R, will therefore depend directly upon the behaviour of ΔDA.[23*]

2.34 *Conclusions*

The model which has been developed here as MFF is no more complicated than ODM. And it has two distinct advantages. In the first place, it provides an analytical framework in which all the main macroeconomic statistics of an open economy – the national income and expenditure accounts, the balance of payments accounts, and the balance sheets of the monetary system – have an obvious place. Second, it disguises no important theoretical problems, in the way that ODM does. If economic activity falls below its full employment level, MFF places the responsibility either upon the downward inflexibility of prices or upon the dynamics of the process by which output moves when it is not in equilibrium: it is thus compatible with both of the two main contemporary interpretations of *The General Theory*.

But MFF has powerful implications which are not to be found in ODM, in particular about the relationship between domestic credit expansion and the balance of payments, and the relationship between the effective exchange rate and the equilibrium level of domestic prices. Are they right, and are they important?

Again, the answer must be an empirical one. It hinges upon whether stable parameters for behavioural equations such as MFF's demand for money and import functions can be identified from past experience, and used with confidence for future prediction of the behaviour of a national economy's balance of payments, inflation rate and level of economic activity.

NOTES

[1] OECD, *Techniques of Economic Forecasting* (OECD, 1965).

[2] Keynes, *The General Theory*, ch. 8.

[3*] For simplicity, all the behavioural relationships in this chapter are assumed to be proportional relationships between variables. Of course, Keynes's 'fundamental law' was not a strictly proportional (or even strictly linear) relationship between consumption and income. But no serious theoretical problems are hidden from view by the simple assumption of proportionality, at least in the context of a short run model.

[4*] The logic of this is that consumption depends upon *income*, and that the value of domestic income must necessarily equal the value of domestic output. There is however a problem here in the case of an open economy. The real value of domestic

* Footnotes marked with an asterisk contain explanations and qualifications which may be neglected by the reader who is interested merely in the broad structure of the argument.

income in terms of goods and services which are *bought* (which is the 'real income' that determines consumption) is not usually the same as 'real output': for the former is the level of nominal income Y, deflated by a price index of domestic residents' expenditure P_A; whereas the latter is Y deflated by a price index of domestic output P_Y. For this reason, the consumption functions employed by economic forecasters in practice have to be rather more complicated than equation ODM 2 explicitly incorporating prices as well as quantities. But once again, no serious theoretical issues are raised by this practical difficulty, which is generally neglected in textbooks.

[5*] Given the identity $Y \equiv C + I + X - M$ and a linear import function $M = a + bY$, it follows by substitution that

$$M = \frac{a}{1+b} + \frac{b}{1+b} \cdot (C + I + X).$$

[6*] Two exceptions to this generalization may be noted. First, it is common practice in balance of payments forecasting to take account of interdependency between $[X]$ and P_X/R on the one hand, and m and P_X/R on the other. These interdependencies are usually described as the 'price-elasticity of supply of exports' and 'price-elasticity of demand for imports' respectively: more will be said about them in later footnotes. Second, in larger economies the assumption that P_X and P_M are determined exogenously may need to be modified: if an economy has significant market power in the markets upon which it trades, its terms of trade (that is, P_X/P_M) may be influenced by its choice of R.

[7*] This extension of ODM to include a monetary system is generally referred to as the 'IS–LM model'.

[8*] Like every generalization about *The General Theory*, this one has been challenged – in this instance by Leijonhufvud, in A. Leijonhufvud, *Keynes and the Classics* (Institute of Economic Affairs, 1971). A real balance effect upon consumption is indeed acknowledged in *The General Theory*, for example on pp. 92–3. But its important theoretical implications are not pursued, and it therefore seems fair to say that it is neglected.

[9*] This point can easily be grasped in terms of a difference equation approach: as has already been pointed out, a difference equation may have an equilibrium value, but its parameters may be such that this value will never be reached. In the difference equation in Section 2.22, the equilibrium value of $[Y]$ will not be reached if the absolute value of $(c - m)$ is greater than 1. Leijonhufvud's interpretation of Keynes's model is of course much more complicated than this, but the principle is the same.

[10] J. Pen, *Modern Economics* (Penguin, 1965), p. 169.

[11] Keynes, *The General Theory*, pp. 262–3.

[12*] The logic of this argument is that domestic production will be allocated between domestic and foreign markets in accordance with the *relative* prices prevailing on those markets, and domestic expenditures will be distributed between imports and domestic production in accordance with their *relative* prices, to the extent that substitution possibilities exist. It is of course this logic which underlies the concepts of a price-elasticity of supply of exports and a price-elasticity of demand for imports, which were referred to in footnote [6*] above.

[13] J. Viner, *Studies in the Theory of International Trade* (Harper and Bros, 1937), ch. 2.

[14] J. J. Polak, 'Monetary Analysis of Income Formation and Payments Problems', *IMF Staff Papers*, vol. VI (1957). Polak's model is formally identical to MFF, except that in the former the time period is chosen such that $k = 1$ in equation MFF 2, whereas in MFF the length of the time period is left open.

[15] H. G. Johnson and J. A. Frenkel (eds.), *The Monetary Approach to the Balance of Payments* (Allen and Unwin, 1976) – in particular the papers in this volume by Mundell and Johnson.

[16]*(This footnote is rather difficult. It assumes a knowledge of material contained later in the chapter, so the reader may prefer to leave it on one side for the time being. It also assumes a knowledge of the concept of an 'elasticity of substitution', which is explained in intermediate rather than introductory textbooks of microeconomics.)

My reason for disliking the terminology is that it is not usually clear, when 'price-elasticities of demand for imports' are measured in practice, precisely what theoretical concept is being measured.

The need for some such term arises, as suggested in footnote [12]*, because it is reasonable to expect some substitution between imports $[M]$ and domestically produced goods $[D]$ when their relative prices change. Let us therefore begin, for the sake of argument, by defining the price-elasticity of demand for imports to be zero when no substitution possibilities exist – that is, when $[M]$ and $[D]$ must be absorbed in fixed proportions.

What will happen, now, if the domestic price of imports P_M/R rises? Purchases of $[M]$ and $[D]$ can continue unchanged only if the domestic monetary authorities are able and willing to permit an expansion of domestic credit. If they are not, both $[M]$ and $[D]$ must fall. It follows that if one attempts to measure the responsiveness of $[M]$ to change in P_M/R without correcting for changes in domestic credit, one is measuring an arbitrary combination of substitution between $[M]$ and $[D]$ and the discretionary behaviour of the monetary authorities. If on the other hand one does correct for changes in domestic credit, a given change in P_M will *always* lead to an exactly offsetting change in $[M]$, with total spending on imports remaining constant. This is true *whatever the substitution possibilities are:* it is $[D]$, not $[M]$, which these will affect.

The only case in which no ambiguity of this kind arises is when the elasticity of substitution between $[M]$ and $[D]$ is unity. In this case, total spending on M and D separately will be independent of the absolute and relative prices of $[M]$ and $[D]$. It is this case which is assumed, for simplicity, in equation MFF 3. Hence, I prefer to describe the underlying assumption as a unit elasticity of substitution between $[M]$ and $[D]$, rather than as a unit price-elasticity of demand for $[M]$.

[17]* If one asks how 'money' should be defined in this context, the answer is implicit in equation MFF 2: MO is that stock of financial assets which one expects domestic residents to hold as some stable function of their income. For present purposes it is assumed to consist of cash and deposits with commercial banks.

[18]* DCE is sometimes referred to as an 'adjusted money stock concept', and *defined* as $\Delta MO - \Delta FR$. These practices reflect a rather strange reluctance on the part of some economists to regard any monetary aggregate other than the money stock as being under the control of the authorities.

[19]* Once again, it is necessary to note that for the equilibrium value of Y to be approached in a stable manner it is necessary that $k/(k + m)$ should lie between 0 and 1. Only if k or m are negative can this fail to be the case – a possibility which is of no practical interest.

[20]* The careful reader will note that we are now treating $[X]$ rather than X as being exogenously determined.

[21]* The equilibrium level of P_A is

$$\frac{P_M}{m \ R}\left(\frac{[X] \ P_X - m \ [X] \ P_X + [F] + R \ \Delta DA}{[Y] \ P_M - m[Y] \ P_M - [X] P_M + m \ [X] \ P_M + [X]P_X - m \ [X] \ P_X + [F] + R \ \Delta DA}\right)$$

where $[F]$ is defined as net capital inflow in foreign currency terms.

[22]* It must be emphasized that this is simply a definition, introduced for theoretical purposes. It is not being suggested here that a 'flexible exchange rate' in the real world will always ensure that $X + F - M = 0$.

[23]* P_A is not however the same as P_Y, and the former may be influenced, in addition, by changes in the terms of trade, P_X/P_M. Thus, a rate of domestic credit expansion which is equal to the growth of domestic output is not sufficient to maintain a stable equilibrium level of domestic prices in an open economy.

3 Conventional Wisdoms and Schools of Thought

The ideas of economists and political philosophers, both when they are right and when they are wrong, are more powerful than is commonly understood. Indeed the world is ruled by little else.

J. M. Keynes

3.1 INTRODUCTION

Simple theories about how economies work are essential for systematic thinking about stabilization policy. But for the policy maker who must reach decisions on a day to day basis, usually under pressure and often with very little reliable information at hand about the state of the economy, simple theories are not enough. The policy maker must also make value judgements about the importance which is attached to different objectives, and about the extent to which different instruments may be used; he must decide how these instruments and objectives are related – in other words, which model is most appropriate to an understanding of the courses of action which are open to him; and he must make a judgement about the values of the parameters in his chosen model. At least, he must do these things implicitly, if a particular course of action (or lack of it) is to be defended as a rational response to a specific set of circumstances.

But in general the process of decision-making in matters of economy policy does not look like this description. Instead it is often based upon what may be described as a 'conventional wisdom' – an agreed set of rules of thumb about the appropriate way to respond in different sorts of situation. The function of such a conventional wisdom is to short-circuit the logical requirements of what has been described above as a 'rational' response.

Since these rules of thumb govern the behaviour of policy makers, they often acquire an element of moral force which is not unlike that of religious dogma. But they can also change over time, sometimes rather fundamentally. And this process of change is not arbitrary. It tends to reflect, as Keynes suggested in the passage which appears at the beginning of this chapter, the outcome of struggles between competing 'schools of thought' in the wider community of economists and political philosophers. (However it would be wrong to imagine that the interaction of professional theorists and conventional wisdoms is always a one-way process: in Chapter 2 attention has already been drawn to one example of a theory which has only recently been formally developed, even though its implications have been among the rules of thumb of various conventional wisdoms for many generations.)

The concept of a school of thought, like that of a conventional wisdom, is a rather imprecise one. It serves to draw attention to the fact that throughout the history of controversy between economists on matters of policy there has been a consistent tendency for the protagonists to group themselves self-consciously under rival standards: among the controversies which are touched upon in this chapter, those between the Bullionists and Anti-Bullionists, Currency School and Banking School, and Keynesians and Monetarists are cases in point. However when one sets out to examine in detail the views that are held by particular thinkers, one usually finds a bewildering variety in each camp and considerable overlap between camps. To the historian of ideas it often seems, as Francis Bacon observed in the early years of the seventeenth century, that 'men create oppositions which are not; and put them into new terms so fixed, as whereas the meaning ought to govern the term, the term in effect governeth the meaning'. Schools of thought undoubtedly exist, but it is uncommonly hard to describe them.

However, these unsatisfactory debates are an important part of the mechanism through which new ideas come to be incorporated in conventional wisdoms, and this chapter attempts to describe some of them. It is inevitable that the description will be over-simple: for the reader who wants a a reasonably objective view of the debates to be described, there is no alternative but to consult the original contributions.

3.2 PRE-KEYNESIAN CONVENTIONAL WISDOMS

3.21 *Conventional Wisdoms and Schools of Thought in Britain*

In the nineteenth century Britain's position as the world's 'first industrial nation' made it the centre of international trade and finance. It is not altogether surprising therefore that the early development of modern thinking on the subject of stabilization policy was a predominantly British affair, or that the conventional wisdoms which emerged in Britain spread to many of the countries which followed closely in the steps of Britain's industrial revolution.

The early years of this revolution were a time of influential developments in economic thought. One was David Hume's exposure of the fallacy of Mercantilism – the idea that it is necessary or useful for a government to regulate foreign trade and payments directly in order to achieve a balance of payments surplus and hence (in Hume's day) to accumulate precious metals. Another was the development by Adam Smith of the idea of a competitive economic system as a self-regulating mechanism, guided by an invisible hand in the best interests of all its members taken together. Such ideas implied that there was relatively little that a government could usefully do in the economic sphere beyond laying down a framework of rules within which the competitive mechanism could be allowed to operate, and ensuring that these rules were properly enforced. They dominated the conventional wisdoms of British governments in the nineteenth century.

Most influential among these conventional wisdoms was what has come to be known as the tradition of Gladstonian finance, named after the leading political figure in Britain in the second half of the century, W. E. Gladstone. Roughly speaking this tradition consisted of three connected principles of budgetary policy.

In the first place the tradition insisted that government expenditures should be restricted to the bare minimum that is necessary to provide the laws and institutions required for the efficient operation of a competitive economic system. No need was perceived for a government to provide goods and services on any substantial scale, or to stimulate by its own spending the level of aggregate demand or rate of economic growth. Within the broad tradition there was of course some room for dispute about what precise level of government expenditures corresponded to the desired bare minimum; but at the end of the nineteenth century the actual level of government expenditure in Britain amounted to about 10 per cent of domestic absorption, and this figure may be taken as about the maximum that is consistent with the Gladstonian ideal.

Secondly, taxation was regarded as having no legitimate function other than to redirect resources from the private to the public purse. It was not to be used to modify the signals given to private producers by a competitive market system. This attitude led to a general preference for direct rather than indirect taxation: in particular, Gladstonian finance regarded with abhorrence any deliberate use of import duties to modify the pattern of domestic industry.

Thirdly, the Gladstonian tradition maintained as a moral principle that the government's budget should balance in such a way that government debt should not increase, and indeed that whenever possible outstanding debt from past borrowing should be systematically reduced. Hence, those goods and services whose production by the government was deemed essential would have to be fully paid for by taxation.

These principles left no room for an active stabilization policy of any kind on the part of the fiscal authorities. And this was consistent with the thinking of most economists of the time. For in nineteenth century Britain, all the influential schools of thought on the subject of stabilization policy regarded it as a matter for the Bank of England – a privately-owned institution, which was to remain so until 1945 – rather than for the Treasury. So the debates between major schools of thought in this period centred upon the desirability or otherwise of particular restrictions upon the Bank's freedom of action in monetary management.

In the debate between Bullionists and Anti-Bullionists, the important issue at stake was whether the Bank should be given a legal obligation to exchange British currency freely for gold at a fixed rate of exchange. A gold standard for sterling was statutorily enforced by the Resumption Act of 1819: it was a victory for the Bullionist school.

In the debate between the Currency and Banking Schools later in the century, the important issue was the desirability of formally separating the Bank's management of the national currency from its normal commercial banking business, and the establishment of rules to govern the former. The outcome, in the Bank Charter Act of 1844, was largely a victory for the Currency School's insistence upon separation and rules.

However, it would be wrong to suppose that all economists of the period regarded the government's problem in the field of stabilization policy as simply one of laying down an appropriate set of rules. Throughout the century, an important minority continued to advocate active currency management by the government, to raise prices and economic activity. (Even then this tradition had a long pedigree. John Law, the Scottish financier whose ambitious schemes bankrupted a large part of the French aristocracy in the early eighteenth century, has been described as 'the genuine ancestor of the idea of managed currency, not only in the obvious sense of that term but in the deeper and wider sense in which it spells management of currency and credit as a means of managing the economic process':[1] but Law's claim to this distinction is not unique.) However, such thinkers did not succeed in capturing an influential section of the economic profession in nineteenth century Britain. The dominant schools of thought favoured an automatic system, in which government would deny itself the freedom to act in a discretionary manner in matters of aggregate monetary policy.

Schumpeter has observed that 'the modern mind dislikes this automatism, as much for political as for economic reasons. But most of the economists of the period under scrutiny liked it for precisely the same reasons'.[2] Nineteenth century Britain's preference for an automatic system stemmed from the view that in practice governments could not be trusted to stabilize an economy in the best interests of their members, even though in principle they might be able to do so. Thus an automatic system, based upon the gold standard mechanism, came to be seen as a moral as well as an economic ideal. But its justification always rested upon this somewhat sceptical assessment of the wisdom of governments; and it was therefore vulnerable to a change of view.

3.22   The Currency Board System

There was little that was Gladstonian about the conventional wisdoms which prevailed in the Treasuries of most of Britain's colonies in the early years of the nineteenth century. Here, the natural tendency which had been feared by nineteenth century economists, for governments to spend and borrow up to the hilt, was conspicuously in evidence. In Kenya, for example, the government's share of domestic absorption was about 40 per cent in the early 1920s, and it remained above 25 per cent throughout the country's years as a British colony.

And between 1921 and 1933 over half of the government's spending in Kenya was financed by borrowing, mainly on the London market. Whenever such borrowing was possible for them, colonial governments such as Kenya's tended to regard the spending which it could finance as their duty, in the interests of the development of their territories.

There was however one constraint under which colonial governments, unlike those of an independent country, were obliged to operate in matters of economic policy. They could not borrow at their own discretion from a subservient monetary authority. Indeed, since most of the monetary authorities of Britain's colonies were responsible directly to the British government rather than to the governments of the colonies in which they operated, the latter were denied altogether the possibility of operating an aggregate monetary policy.

The 'currency board system' was developed gradually, and in a trial-and-error manner, in the second half of the nineteenth century and the early years of the twentieth. It reached its simplest and most characteristic form in the currency boards of West Africa (established in 1912) and East Africa (1919). These boards were designed as a practical expression of three main principles. The first was essentially Bullionist in inspiration: the domestic currency of each colony, or group of colonies, was to be freely exchangeable for sterling at a fixed rate of exchange. The second reflected the views of the Currency School in Britain: the boards were to hold a reserve of sterling assets amounting to at least 100 per cent of the value of their domestic currency liabilities. And the third reflected the general presumption of *all* the influential schools of thought in nineteenth century Britain, in favour of automaticity and the abstention of government from currency management: with these two rules established, there was believed to be no need for active monetary regulation in colonial territories, so that the functions of the boards could be confined to money-changing and the relatively straightforward matter of deciding the precise form in which to hold their sterling assets.

In practice the ideal of automaticity was achieved neither in Britain nor in its colonies. In Britain, central banking was developed by the Bank of England, within the framework of rules to which it was subject, into a complex and mysterious art. In Britain's colonies, no currency board remained as passive as the above simplified description suggests that they were intended to do. But in Britain until 1931, and in its colonies until much later, active intervention by the monetary authorities was guided by what had become fundamental articles of faith: that the exchange rate was sacrosanct; and that there was practically nothing that the authorities could usefully do to influence the level of prices or economic activity.

3.3 THE KEYNESIAN REVOLUTION IN STABILIZATION POLICY

J. M. Keynes's first major work, *Indian Currency and Finance*, played an important part in influencing the form which was given to the currency board of

West Africa, and later of East Africa. But throughout his life Keynes adopted a much more optimistic view of the potential benefits to be derived from an active stabilization policy than the view which was enshrined in the conventional wisdom of his day. In the 1920s and 1930s he set about assaulting this conventional wisdom. He succeeded, perhaps even beyond his expectations, in creating a quite different one.

In his *A Tract on Monetary Reform*,[3] published in 1923, Keynes assumed without argument that the choice of instruments and objectives of economic policy should be made in practical, not moral terms. The central issue which Keynes posed in this book was whether 'external stability' (that is, a fixed exchange rate for the domestic currency) or 'internal stability' (that is, a stable equilibrium level of domestic prices) is a more useful objective for the monetary authorities to pursue. This question presupposes that the two possibilities will, in certain circumstances, be *alternatives* – an implication which can readily be derived from model MFF in Chapter 2, but not from ODM. (Indeed, MFF is in its essentials the model which underlies Keynes's *Tract*.)

Of the two possibilities, Keynes came down firmly in favour of internal stability. He did so because when prices are in practice inflexible downwards a fall in the equilibrium level of domestic prices entails a decline in the level of economic activity – something which, as was suggested in Chapter 1, Keynes took to be an evil that the authorities should do all in their power to avoid. The argument of the *Tract*, therefore, was that Britain's monetary authorities should vary the effective exchange rate of sterling in such a way as to prevent the equilibrium level of domestic prices from falling.

In political terms this argument was a failure. Two years after the *Tract* was published Britain's Chancellor of the Exchequer, W. S. Churchill, announced that Britain was returning to the gold standard (which had been abandoned as a result of war in 1914) at an exchange rate which entailed in practice a substantial fall in the equilibrium domestic price level. The prevailing conventional wisdom declined to accept responsibility for the fall in economic activity which followed. Keynes protested in vain against *The Economic Consequences of Mr Churchill*. If he was to succeed in overthrowing the conventional wisdom, he needed a theory which placed responsibility for the fall in economic activity firmly upon the action which the authorities had taken, rather than upon transitory inflexibilities in the adjustment process; and he needed a school of thought to support his argument. Hence *The General Theory*, which Keynes regarded a year before he completed it as 'a book on economic theory which will largely revolutionize – not, I suppose, at once but in the course of the next ten years – the way the world thinks about economic problems'.[4]

His new theory took the form of a model of an economy closed to foreign trade – for, as suggested in Chapter 2, Keynes was well aware that his claim to have removed responsibility for variations in economic activity from price inflexibilities could not be sustained in the case of an open economy. So the exchange rate was not among the policy variables which were considered in *The General Theory*. Equally surprising to those readers who were familiar with his earlier work, perhaps, was the fact that Keynes no longer seemed to regard a central bank's influence upon monetary aggregates as being particularly important. Instead, it was upon aggregate *fiscal* policy that he now placed the main responsibility for ensuring a full employment level of economic activity:

> The State will have to exercise a guiding influence on the propensity to consume partly through its scheme of taxation, partly by fixing the rate of interest, and partly, perhaps, in other ways. Furthermore, it seems unlikely that the influence of banking policy on the rate of interest will be sufficient by itself to determine an optimum rate of investment. I conceive, therefore, that a somewhat comprehensive socialization of investment will prove the only means of securing an approximation to full employment.[5]

However, Keynes maintained a belief in the virtues of the market mechanism as a means of deciding how a *given* total of goods and services should be allocated: the State's important function, in his view, was simply to ensure that this total was a full-employment total.

As summarized in these paragraphs, Keynes's view was a complex mixture of value judgements, theoretical propositions and assumptions about the values of particular parameters in the economic system. It seems reasonable to regard the following brief list of propositions as essentially 'Keynesian':

> K.1. A high level of economic activity cannot be ensured without active government regulation of the economy.

> K.2. The maintenance of a high level of economic activity should be a primary concern of government.

> K.3. A high level of activity can in general be achieved by the careful regulation of the aggregate level of government expenditures, and tax rates – that is, by aggregate fiscal policy.

> K.4. As an instrument of policy, *aggregate* fiscal policy is to be preferred to policies which involve more detailed and discriminatory intervention in the economy.

This provisional list makes no mention of inflation or the balance of payments among the concerns of stabilization policy, or of the exchange rate among its instruments. On these other matters, the views of the school of thought which grew up around *The General Theory*, and which it is reasonable to describe as Keynesian, are rather more diverse.

In the first place it is recognized that in an open economy, the regulation of economic activity through aggregate fiscal policy will affect the current account of the balance of payments, and that the corollary of a high level of activity may be a current account balance which is inadequate to match the desired or attainable level of capital receipts and payments. The result will then be a balance of payments deficit for an economy with a fixed exchange rate, or a depreciation of the currency if the exchange rate is allowed to float. Both tend to be regarded by Keynesians as undesirable – the former for the logical reason that it cannot be sustained indefinitely, the latter for the practical reason that it will mean a rise in import prices in domestic currency terms. When confronted with such a dilemma, the general response of Keynesian economists, in line with proposition K.2, has been to favour devaluation or depreciation of the currency. But in this area, widely differing views have persisted within the Keynesian school.

Second, the school contains many different shades of opinion about the most appropriate method of controlling inflation. Until about the middle of the 1960s, the dominant view was that those fiscal and monetary policies which influence the level of economic activity *also* determine, in large measure, the rate of inflation – or at least that part of it which is generated domestically. Indeed, one of the main attractions of the Phillips curve to economists of the Keynesian school was the fact that it appeared to offer a precise menu from which policy makers could select that combination of economic activity and domestically generated inflation which they preferred. But since the mid-1960s there has been a marked shift of emphasis among Keynesians, at least in the UK. To increasing numbers, the link between economic activity and the rate of inflation has come to seem a tenuous one; as a result, various forms of direct controls upon wages and prices have come to be seen by many Keynesians as necessary if governments are to be able to control the rate of inflation.

The reader will have noted many points of tangency between this brief account of the views (and disagreements) of Keynesian economists, and the account which was provided in the previous chapter of model ODM. This is, of course, no accident. For whether or not that model reasonably represents what Keynes had to say in *The General Theory*, its essential function in introductory textbooks is to instruct the student in the doctrines of a Keynesian conventional wisdom; for its implications are the beliefs of the Keynesian school. The model provides the policy maker with a list of what he needs to know in order to manage an economy in Keynesian manner. For the single most important feature of the conventional wisdom which Keynes succeeded in substituting for those that had gone before was the view that an economy *needs* to be consciously managed to achieve any chosen set of objectives. Automatic mechanisms were seen by Keynes as simply not sufficient.

3.4 CHALLENGES TO THE KEYNESIAN SCHOOL

As a conventional wisdom, Keynesianism has been attacked at many points and from many directions. Those on the political Left object to its general presumption in favour of market mechanisms; those on the political Right are suspicious of its belief in active government management of the economy, with the degree of government power over the individual that this entails. But the challenges which are briefly outlined in this section are much more limited in scope. They are those that have been mounted by other economists, sharing the same theoretical tradition as Keynes and his followers and roughly the same set of value judgements about the proper objectives of stabilization policy.

3.41 *Monetarism*

The most influential of these challenges has come from a group of economists led by Milton Friedman of the University of Chicago. This group has become a distinctive school of thought in its own right, describing itself as Monetarist.

The Chicago challenge began in the 1950s in a relatively restrained manner. In the first instance it was a growing insistence, based upon detailed and painstaking study of historical data, that the money : income ratio k was not as unpredictable as Keynes and his immediate followers had supposed. Moderately refined versions of the old Cambridge demand-for-money equation appeared to fit quite well in many empirical applications in a wide variety of countries and historical periods. Next, Friedman and his colleagues turned to a detailed examination of the historical record in the USA; and they reached the con- clusion – among many others – that fluctuations in the money stock were a reflection of the actions of the US monetary authorities.

Some Keynesians contested the conclusions reached in this empirical work. But the Keynesian school as a whole could absorb such findings without serious difficulties; and on the whole it did so in the course of the 1960s. Money, and monetary policy, came gradually to be seen as rather more important in influen- cing the behaviour of 'real' national economies than they had seemed to Keynes in 1936. But this was a relatively minor change of emphasis, which the Keyne- sian school could easily accommodate within its model of the economy merely by modifying its beliefs about the value and predictability of some of the model's parameters.

Friedman and his colleagues did not stop at this point, however. They turned next in their empirical work to an assault upon the stability and predictability of the Keynesian multiplier. The assault was not conclusive, as indeed it could not be: for in economics the evidence concerning the stability or instability of a par- ticular relationship can never be complete. But in attacking a relationship which occupies such a fundamental position in the characteristic model of the Keyne- sian school, Friedman necessarily espoused a quite different view about the way in which macroeconomic variables are determined.

With some simplification, this view may be summarized in three propositions:

M.1. Nominal income Y depends on an exogenously determined money stock, a stable demand-for-money function, and nothing else of any importance.

M.2. A change in nominal income always *follows* a change in the money stock, and in a definite manner: changes in MO are followed in the first instance by sympathetic changes in output; but this effect is temporary, and as it subsides the effect of the change in MO shifts permanently to the general level of prices.

M.3. In the long run, output moves towards equilibrium at what we have called its full employment level, of its own accord, whatever monetary or fiscal policy the authorities pursue.

In Chapter 2 it was pointed out that proposition M.1 can easily be derived from a very simple formal model of a closed economy; and a strong theoretical case can be made out for proposition M.3, in any economy in which prices are free to move downwards as well as upwards. These two propositions logically imply the third. It is important to note, however, that the strength of these propositions in the minds of members of the Monetarist school is not derived from theoretical reasoning, but rather from the way in which these economists interpret a very large volume of empirical evidence. A large part of this evidence – though by no means all of it – is drawn from the experience of the USA.

Finally, most Monetarists follow Friedman in subscribing to a fourth proposition:

> M.4. In practice the time-lags between changes in money, output and prices are of unpredictable length, so that the authorities cannot *control* changes in the level of economic activity with the only instrument that allows them to *influence* this variable – namely, changes in the stock of money.

This fourth proposition implies that governments which attempt to control economic activity in the short term are bound to fail in practice. Most Monetarists believe it would be better if they did not try. In Friedman's words, 'Our present understanding of the relation between money, prices and output is so meagre, that there is so much leeway in these relations, that . . . discretionary changes do more harm than good'.[6]

3.42 *Open-economy Monetarism*

The propositions which were outlined in the previous section obviously cannot be derived from either of our two simple models of an open economy. True, the Monetarist school shares with MFF's equation MFF 2 an assertion of the predictability, if not the exact constancy, of k. And it shares too the behavioural assumption which was added, in equation MFF 6, that output will tend in equilibrium towards its full employment level. But the Monetarist propositions differ from MFF in treating the money stock, rather than domestic credit, as an exogenous variable. Is this an important difference?

To begin with, it may be recalled from our discussion in Chapter 2 that there is one case in which this particular difference vanishes. If the exchange rate is 'perfectly flexible', in a precise sense of this term, changes in domestic credit and changes in the money stock are identical. MFF then becomes, in effect, a model of a closed economy; and it is a model which implies the first three of the four Monetarist propositions which have been outlined. (It is difficult to conceive of any theoretical model – certainly, any simple model – which could imply the fourth.)

Now it is fair to note that many Monetarists, including Friedman, favour a regime of flexible rather than fixed exchange rates. But the central propositions of Monetarism are an assertion about what the world is like, not an assertion about what it would be like in specific circumstances or about what it ought to be like. And according to MFF, this assertion is false for a small, open economy on a fixed exchange rate. For according to MFF the authorities in such an economy cannot in principle control the stock of money without *necessarily* controlling everything else: changes in the money stock are the result of changes in other variables rather than their cause. The question whether money or domestic credit is to be regarded as exogenous is therefore a question of some importance.

If however one substitutes 'domestic credit' for 'money' in the first three propositions of Monetarism, one arrives at a view of the world which corresponds almost exactly to the implications of MFF. It seems reasonable to describe this view as open-economy Monetarism. There is no self-conscious school of thought which places itself under this banner. But it seems fair to describe the prescriptions which the International Monetary Fund typically seeks to impose upon those governments which borrow from it as being derived from an open-economy Monetarist view. It is no accident that a formal model similar to MFF was first developed by the Fund's economists.

3.43   *The New Cambridge School*

The final challenge to the Keynesian school to be considered here is a very recent development, by what is still a small group confined to the Department of Applied Economics in the University of Cambridge. It is possible that in ten years' time few economists will have heard of the New Cambridge school. But it is of interest here, as a criticism of the conventional Keynesian wisdom which has grown up in the citadel of Keynesian economics.

The initial concern of what has become the New Cambridge school was an attempt to devise a framework for planning public expenditure in the UK in the 'medium term' – that is, over a five year time horizon. From its origins in the late 1960s, the group's focus of attention was therefore what was described in Chapter 1 as aggregate fiscal policy.

The group was strongly affected by, and itself contributed to, a growing belief among British economists that the discretionary changes in government expenditure and tax changes which had been practised in accordance with conventional Keynesian wisdom in the UK had turned out, on the whole, to have been badly timed. This belief led to an interest in the kind of rules of thumb for fiscal policy which might lead to a better outcome; and this interest led in turn to a reassessment of the way in which aggregate fiscal policy – and later, other instruments of policy too – affect the economy.

For present purposes, the New Cambridge school's characteristic beliefs about how the British economy works may be summarized as follows:

NC.1. Aggregate fiscal policy (that is, the level of government spending, tax rates, and the consequent government financial deficit) affects the behaviour of the balance of payments. It does not affect the level of economic activity, except perhaps temporarily.

NC.2 Economic activity may be controlled by variations in the effective exchange rate (or by import restrictions, which the New Cambridge school regards as a preferable alternative with roughly similar effects).

These implications cannot be derived from a model like ODM without considerable intellectual ingenuity. But they *can* be derived in a relatively straightforward manner from MFF. In the first place, as the New Cambridge school has come to realize, proposition NC.1 follows from an assumption that the private sector's demand for *financial assets* is a stable function of money income. This is clearly very close – though not quite identical – to MFF's assumption that the private sector's demand for *money* is a stable function of income. Thus, the school shares MFF's conclusion that aggregate fiscal policy has a simple and direct effect upon the balance of payments, and it is essentially the same logic that leads to this conclusion.

The second proposition can be derived from MFF even more straightforwardly if one substitutes for equation MFF 6 an assumption that the prices of domestically produced goods are completely inflexible, and must be regarded as exogenous to the system. For MFF will then yield, not a theory of the equilibrium level of *prices* (as it did in Chapter 2), but instead a theory of the equilibrium level of economic activity: and this latter theory corresponds exactly to the second major proposition of the New Cambridge school.

3.5 CONCLUSION

It has been argued in this chapter that the theoretical approach of standard economics textbooks (namely, model ODM and its various extensions) is a reflection of the beliefs of a Keynesian school of thought which has become a Keynesian conventional wisdom on matters of stabilization policy; and that this conventional wisdom is now under attack from several directions. Two important and apparently quite different assaults upon it can be explained straightforwardly in terms of a simple model – a model which Keynes himself used in his early work, and the origins of which can be traced at least as far back as the early years of the eighteenth century.

The implication is clear. If one wishes to understand contemporary debate on problems of stabilization policy, a working knowledge of the *single* macroeconomic model which is expounded in contemporary textbooks is not enough: for it is precisely the practical usefulness of this textbook model that is in dispute.

In these first three chapters our concern has been with general concepts, theories, schools of thought and conventional wisdoms. In the second part of the book, our concern is the relevance of this general 'bundle of ideas' to the experience of a single country, Kenya, in its first ten years of political independence.

NOTES

[1] J. A. Schumpeter, *History of Economic Analysis* (Allen and Unwin, 1954), p. 322.
[2] Ibid., p. 732.
[3] J. M. Keynes, *A Tract on Monetary Reform* (Macmillan, 1923).
[4] M. Stewart, *Keynes and After*, 2nd ed. (Penguin, 1972), p. 12.
[5] Keynes, *The General Theory*, p. 378.
[6] M. Friedman, *The Counter-Revolution in Monetary Theory* (Institute of Economic Affairs, 1970), p. 26.

Part 2

THE KENYAN EXPERIENCE

The Road of Excess leads to the Palace of Wisdom, for you cannot know what is enough until you know what is more than enough.

William Blake

4 Instruments and Objectives in the Kenyan Context

An essential ingredient of economic independence is the ability of a country to formulate and execute her own economic and social policies.

Mwai Kibaki

4.1 BACKGROUND

4.11 *Aggregate Fiscal Policy in the Colonial Period*

The currency board monetary system which was described in general terms in Chapter 3 kept the colonial government in Kenya on a very tight rein.

In the first place the government could not use the exchange rate as an instrument of policy. In practice, the only way in which the effective exchange rate could be altered was by a change in the rates of commission which the East African Currency Board charged for converting East African currency into sterling, and vice versa. This weapon was in fact used on several occasions. But it was confined, by the Currency Board's regulations, within very narrow limits. And it was exercised, not by the authorities in Kenya, but by a Board which consisted until 1960 of a small group of part-time officials in London, responsible directly to the British Secretary of State for the Colonies.

Second, neither the Board nor the colonial authorities could bring any significant influence to bear upon the aggregate lending behaviour of the commercial banks which operated in Kenya. For the domestic monetary system's guarantee of free convertibility into sterling at a fixed rate of exchange allowed commercial banks to treat colonial territories as extensions of the British financial system. There was no reason why their lending and deposits in any single colonial territory should bear a particular relationship to one another. The 'big three' banks which operated in Kenya in the colonial period – Barclays Bank DCO, National and Grindlays, and the Standard Bank – were all British banks with head offices in London. The interest rates which they charged for advances and paid on deposits in Kenya were directly related to, and determined by, interest rates in London; the amount of lending which they undertook in Kenya was governed by the number of safe lending opportunities which they perceived locally, given this level of interest rates; and their local deposits depended upon what Kenyan residents chose to hold. The ratio of local advances to local deposits could therefore vary widely, and in Kenya it did so during the colonial period.

Third, throughout most of this period the Currency Board was not allowed to hold in its currency reserve fund the securities of the Kenya government, so the fiscal authorities were given no latitude to 'print money'. This restriction was lifted in December 1955; but as long as the East African Currency Board remained in existence, strict limits were placed upon the government's access to this source of funds.

These three restrictions did not entirely prevent the colonial government in Kenya from attempting to stabilize the economy, if it chose to do so. If it wished, the government could vary its resort to funds borrowed on the London market in a contra-cyclical manner – at least to the extent that such funds were available at acceptable rates of interest. In general, however, it made little attempt to follow such a policy. When it was possible for the colonial government to borrow from the London market, it borrowed, and spent the proceeds. There was no systematic attempt to use for stabilization purposes the important, although limited, instruments which it possessed.

Now, it is easy to rationalize this deliberate choice in terms of MFF. For the currency board system effectively guaranteed the free convertibility of domestic currency into sterling at a fixed exchange rate. This removed from the authorities in Kenya any need to worry about the state of the balance of payments: indeed, no official balance of payments estimates were presented for Kenya during the colonial period. Hence, according to MFF, the most that the Kenyan authorities could lose by renouncing the use of the budget for stabilization purposes would be an essentially *temporary* influence upon prices or economic activity. It could reasonably be argued that such a game was simply not worth the candle.

But when the world is viewed through the spectacles of ODM, this choice by the colonial authorities becomes less easy to justify. And the gradual encroachment of Keynesian ideas upon the Kenya Treasury from about 1950 onwards led to a serious questioning of the earlier approach. For example, the economy was acknowledged by the authorities to be in a state of recession in the late 1950s, and again in the two years before political independence was achieved in 1963; and it was recognized on these occasions that aggregate fiscal policy was tending to make the recessions even deeper than they might otherwise have been. By this time, however, it was too late for second thoughts. By the beginning of the 1960s the government in Kenya was heavily dependent upon financial support from the British Treasury not only for its development expenditure, but also to finance its recurrent budget. And this was a situation which neither the British Treasury nor an independent government in Kenya could tolerate for long after independence had been achieved. Whatever the conventional wisdom might be, economic stabilization had to take second place.

4.12   *Monetary Policy in the Last Years of the Currency Board*

In principle, political independence meant the removal of all restraints upon the use of instruments of policy. But in practice it was not until two years after independence that the Kenya government began to forge for itself new instruments with which to control the short run behaviour of the economy. For in the early 1960s it was widely hoped, not least by Kenya's leaders, that the newly independent countries of East Africa would be able to form some kind of political federation. And as long as these hopes persisted monetary policy was entrusted to the East African Currency Board, to be developed on an East African basis.

In anticipation of the changes which independence would bring the commercial banks in Kenya, by 1960 or perhaps even earlier, began to regulate their local lending in accordance with their local deposit liabilities. But they did so in rather difficult circumstances, for the transition to independence was accompanied by several rather sudden reductions in the level of deposits and by emergency demands upon their total resources which the banks could not easily refuse. Thus local liquidity ratios in Kenya in the early 1960s were generally much lower than the banks would have liked; and the result was that fairly severe credit rationing was maintained throughout these years.

At the same time, the East African Currency Board began to develop and exercise an influence upon the behaviour of the commercial banks. Its first concern was to create a local market for the Treasury Bills and other short term securities of the East African governments, and also for some private short term securities. By allowing the market interest rate and its own rediscount rate to be set at levels which made such paper a slightly more profitable liquid investment for the commercial banks than similar assets in London, the Board was able to create a continuing demand. And it had no difficulty in persuading the Treasuries of Uganda and Tanzania to supply the new market with securities. (Between 1960 and 1965 the Kenya government was reluctant to issue short term securities despite the demand which the Board had created, for reasons that will be explained later in this chapter.)

The commercial banks then readily adopted the convention that their interest rates in East Africa were set on the basis of rates prevailing in the local money market, rather than on the basis of London rates. Up to the end of 1963 this change remained of no practical significance, for rates in the East African market fluctuated in step with those in London, and the Currency Board signalled its willingness to allow them to do so by varying its rediscount rates accordingly. In 1963, however, the Board gave warning in its Annual Report, at a time when interest rates in London were falling, that 'it is consistent with the beginnings of an independent monetary policy that there should not always be automatic adjustment'. The Board's first major act of monetary policy was, indeed, to drive a wedge between interest rates in East Africa and those in London. When the latter rose sharply in February 1964 the Board intervened to prevent interest rates in East Africa from rising in sympathy; and when London rates rose even further in November, the Board intervened once again – this time to *lower* interest rates in East Africa.

However, free convertibility of East African currency into sterling was at first maintained. The emergence of a significant interest rate differential therefore created a considerable incentive for liquid funds to be switched from East Africa to London, both directly (with firms and individuals running down their local deposits) and indirectly (with firms switching their short term borrowing as far as possible from London to East Africa). It is difficult to disentangle the effect of this factor from many others that might have contributed to the same result, but there can be little doubt that the interest rate differential deliberately created by the Currency Board was largely responsible for a substantial reduction in the ratio of deposits to income in Kenya, and a corresponding net outflow of capital in 1964 and the early months of 1965. If the commercial banks were to be able to finance any increase in local expenditures – as both the Currency Board and the Kenya government desired – the differential could be preserved only if free convertibility was ended. The desirability of a stable, and low, structure of domestic interest rates remained a central assumption of monetary policy in Kenya throughout the period with which this study is concerned; the imposition of exchange control upon capital transfers was therefore inevitable, and the step was taken in June 1965.

At the same time it was announced that the unified East African monetary system was to be dismantled, with the Currency Board being replaced by separate central banks and monetary systems in each country. The initiative was taken by Tanzania, which had achieved independence earlier than either Uganda or Kenya, and which had felt increasingly severely the restrictions upon its own freedom of action which were necessary in a monetary union. The Kenya government therefore acquired, in 1966, new instruments of stabilization policy for which no pressing need had hitherto been felt, and whose use in a *national* context had not hitherto been seriously contemplated.

4.2 THE EVOLUTION OF OBJECTIVES, 1963–69

In matters of stabilization policy, the first years of Kenya's independence were notable for caution and continuity. There were, it will be suggested, some important objective reasons for this. But the continuity may have owed something, too, to the personality of the man who guided Kenya's initial steps in stabiliza-tion policy between 1962 and 1969 – the Minister for Finance, James Gichuru. The description which follows draws principally upon statements of policy made by Gichuru, particularly in his budget speeches in these years.

4.21 *Aggregate Fiscal Policy*

As has already been noted, development expenditures by the Kenya government were severely restrained by a shortage of finance on the eve of Independence.

Mainly because of the political uncertainties of the period, the government was unable to borrow from the London capital market, or indeed from the small capital market in Nairobi which had been gradually built up in the 1950s. To maintain any development expenditure at all it was obliged to rely upon funds provided by the British Treasury. And this source not only financed almost all of Kenya's development expenditures: it also financed a significant part of the government's *recurrent* spending. In the fiscal year 1962–63, almost 24 per cent of total Kenya government revenues came directly from the British Treasury.

The approach of Independence compounded the problem; after Independence, Kenya's armed forces and diplomatic representation would place new financial burdens upon the government; funds would have to be provided for an intensive training effort as British civil servants were rapidly replaced by Kenyans; and it was inevitable that a popularly elected government would be under strong pressure to increase expenditures, particularly upon development and social services. As a final straw, there loomed the spectre of about 100 million Kenya shillings (K.sh.) worth of debt, incurred in the 1940s and 1950s, which was due to be repaid in 1965.

This fiscal problem was examined in the year before Kenya's Independence by no less than three visiting missions, one of them organized by the World Bank. All three declared the problem to be insoluble in the short run. There was believed to be *some* scope for cutting back expenditure and raising taxes without too serious effects upon an economy which was already believed to be in a state of depression: but the scope was judged to be rather small. Certainly, it did not seem large enough to reduce significantly the acute dependence of the Kenya Treasury upon London. The only strategy that visiting expert opinion felt able to recommend was a gradual, long term solution. This would require considerable restraint and single-mindedness on the part of the Kenyan authorities, together with goodwill on the part of the British government. It was this solution that Gichuru pursued, with remarkable success, in the 1960s.

It involved the persistent application of three strands of budgetary policy. The first was firm Treasury restraint upon the spending ministries. Central government spending as a whole was not allowed to rise significantly as a percentage of monetary GDP once the inevitable costs of Independence had been absorbed: it remained stable at about 30 per cent between 1964 and 1969. ('Restraint' in this particular sense was made relatively painless by the fact that monetary GDP in nominal terms rose at a fairly steady annual rate of about 10 per cent. Even so, persistent vigilance was needed on the part of the Treasury to prevent recurrent expenditures in particular from rising too fast.)

Second, tax rates were increased steadily across the board, so that the ratio of tax revenues to monetary GDP rose gradually from about 20 per cent at the time of Independence to about 25 per cent by the end of the 1960s.

And third, after the imposition of exchange control in 1965 there was a considerable development of government long term borrowing from the domestic capital market, in particular by the issuing of securities to 'captive' financial institutions such as the new National Social Security Fund.

By these means, Gichuru was able to achieve a steady reduction in the dependence of the Kenya Treasury upon external funds not only in relative terms (from 8 per cent of Kenya's monetary GDP in the year after Independence to about 3 per cent by the end of the 1960s) but in absolute terms as well. By 1969 the Treasury was financing the whole of its recurrent budget, and almost two-thirds of its development expenditures, from internal sources. Financial independence had been largely achieved.

The corollary of this achievement was, however, that aggregate fiscal policy could not be and was not used for short term stabilization purposes. Indeed, a systematic reduction in the level of government's overseas borrowing entailed a steady 'deflationary' fiscal stance, unless the government chose to raise its borrowing from the domestic monetary system. Such borrowing was widely advocated in academic circles in the mid-1960s, and even by important members of the Kenya Cabinet. But Gichuru placed the weight of his authority firmly against it. During his years as Minister for Finance, net short term borrowing from the monetary system by the Kenya government was, indeed, negative.

This feature of budgetary policy in the 1960s is to be explained largely in practical terms. Until 1965 the Kenya Treasury was deeply concerned about the impending necessity to redeem or refinance about K.sh. 100 million worth of long term debt. In the process it expected to be obliged to make use of its power to borrow at short term by issuing Treasury Bills to the East African Currency Board or the local money market. In order to avoid serious financial difficulty in 1965, it was therefore careful to keep in reserve about K.sh. 100 million of its borrowing entitlement in the Currency Board; and to do this it was obliged not to issue any short term securities to the Board between 1960 and 1965. When 1965 arrived, however, the imposition of exchange control led to a dramatic and largely unexpected revival of the Nairobi market for long term government securities, which the Treasury chose at once to exploit: short term borrowing from the Currency Board proved to be necessary, in the event, only for a few months at the end of 1965.

After 1965 the circumstances were quite different but the practical consequences were the same. Gichuru's opposition to short term borrowing from the monetary system slackened: in his 1968 budget, for example, he declared that he was 'prepared to take some risks in maintaining the momentum of development expenditure, if necessary, even by resort to short term borrowing'. But by this time the spending ministries were having difficulties in implementing a sufficiently large number of projects to absorb the rapidly rising volume of funds which the Treasury was now providing for them on development account. Despite the change in attitude, net short term borrowing obstinately refused to materialize in the government's financial statements. It was not a situation that could be relied upon to continue indefinitely.

4.22 *Exchange Rate and Monetary Policy*

The Kenyan authorities acquired a Central Bank and a national monetary system largely by default. However the acquisition of new instruments of policy did raise the question of the manner in which they were to be used, in a form that could not be avoided.

The Central Bank of Kenya Act in March 1966 set out the new Bank's objectives in the usual, rather general terms:

> The principal objects of the Bank shall be to regulate the issue of notes and coins, to assist in the development and maintenance of a sound monetary, credit and banking system in Kenya conducive to the orderly and balanced economic development of the country and the external stability of the currency, and to serve as banker and financial adviser to the Government.

In his 1966 budget speech, Gichuru set out the important objectives in a simpler and more forthright manner:

> The ultimate objective of a proper monetary policy ... is to keep the value of the currency stable both in relation to the internal price level and to gold and principal reserve currencies.

The Central Bank of Kenya Act also laid down two specific financial constraints which will prove important later in this story. First, an absolute limit of K.sh. 240 million was placed upon government borrowing from the Bank in any form. (This limit was to be amended and made more flexible at the end of 1972.) Second, a minimum target level was prescribed for the Bank's holdings of foreign exchange:

> The Bank shall at all times use its best endeavours to maintain a reserve of external assets at an aggregate amount of not less than the value of four months' imports as recorded and averaged for the last three preceding years.

In 1966 exchange rate stability seemed a straightforward concept. Kenya's shilling had been at par with the British shilling since 1921, and the goal of 'stability' was undoubtedly assumed to imply that it should remain so. But in November 1967 the ambiguity of the concept was made clear when Britain devalued its currency. The Kenyan authorities decided not to follow this devaluation, but to establish instead a new parity with sterling. The decision entailed an appreciation of the shilling's effective exchange rate by about 5 per cent.

There are two important points to be made about this action of policy. The first is that it was taken in conjunction with the authorities of Tanzania and Uganda. A uniform exchange rate policy was in practice an important feature of the East African Community. Indeed, as the years passed the exchange rate came to be almost the only common element of policy in the Community, and hence a matter of increasing symbolic importance. In 1971, for example, the Kenyan authorities were prepared to sacrifice what appears to have been their best judgement about the appropriate exchange rate, when the Tanzanian authorities insisted upon a different policy. This reflected, in part, a belief that the exchange rate is a rather less important instrument of national stabilization than are aggregate fiscal and monetary policies – a belief to which we shall return in later chapters.

Second, the Kenyan authorities did nevertheless take great care in November 1967 to examine the economic implications of the decision with which they were confronted by the devaluation of sterling. The main national considerations in favour of the decision that was actually taken were two in number. First, a devaluation with sterling would have led to an undesirable increase in domestic prices, and second, the healthy balance of payments situation in Kenya in 1966 and the early part of 1967 provided no positive arguments in favour of a devaluation. Against this, it was recognized that an appreciation of the shilling would have harmful effects upon the earnings of the agricultural sector, and perhaps also upon the level of economic activity: but it was judged that these were risks worth taking.

The immediate effect of the decision was a tendency for the business community to accelerate its payments for imports and to delay the remittance of its export earnings in the expectation that a devaluation of the shilling might later be forced upon the authorities. These changes in the 'leads and lags' of foreign payments were financed by a withdrawal of deposits from the commercial banks and by an increase in advances: the banks' liquidity position thus deteriorated rapidly in the early months of 1968. As a result, the foreign assets of the monetary system fell sharply below the Central Bank's minimum target.

This was diagnosed by the Bank, however, as an essentially temporary phenomenon which would reverse itself in due course. The Bank did take some positive steps – reducing its own rediscounts, prohibiting inter-bank lending, and introducing forward cover for foreign exchange transactions – but in general its policy (as described in its 1968 Annual Report) was the passive one of 'letting the diminishing liquidity of the banking system have its full impact on their willingness and capacity to lend'. The commercial banks' advances : deposits ratios were in fact rapidly restored to the 'normal' levels that had prevailed in 1966–67, and the decline in Kenya's reserves of foreign exchange was reversed without any need for the Central Bank to prescribe a minimum liquid assets ratio. Indeed, the Bank did not acquire the legal power to impose such a ratio upon the commercial banks until 1968.

But for the rest of the 1960s the Bank had no need for this weapon of policy. Commercial bank advances to the private sector remained virtually static until the early months of 1970, with the banks becoming increasingly liquid. Far from wishing to restrict credit, the Central Bank suggested in its 1969 Annual Report that it 'would have welcomed a higher rate of increase in bank advances than was actually taking place'. Its techniques of control gave it no power to bring about such an increase: monetary policy therefore remained passive throughout the remainder of the 1960s.

4.3   NEW DEPARTURES IN STABILIZATION POLICY, 1970–73

In 1970 Kenya embarked upon a much more positive phase in the development of stabilization policy. The change coincided with the publication in December 1969 of a new Development Plan for the years 1970–74; with the replacement of James Gichuru as Minister for Finance by Mwai Kibaki – a man who brought the skills of an academic economist to the office, as well as the experience of a ministerial career in two other economic ministries; and finally, in November 1970, with the amalgamation under Kibaki's direction of the Ministries of Finance and Economic Planning.

4.31   *The Fiscal Experiment, 1970–71*

The new Development Plan gave a clear indication that a change in the direction of aggregate fiscal policy was in prospect. In the first place, it announced that 'Government proposes to raise the level of its own spending at a faster rate than was the case during the first Plan', with new initiatives particularly in the industrial sector. In the second place, when the pattern of financing proposed by the Plan is compared with the actual pattern of government revenues in Kenya in the late 1960s, some important differences are evident. First, it was proposed to raise the level of external finance substantially, from less than 8 per cent of government expenditure in the fiscal year 1968–69 to about 13 per cent in the new Plan period. Second, it was proposed that 3.5 per cent of government revenue should be obtained from the monetary system by means of Treasury Bill issues and direct borrowing from the central Bank. Furthermore, since the higher level of external borrowing was by no means certain to be achieved at least in the early years of the Plan, *additional* borrowing from the monetary system was envisaged as an appropriate method of dealing with any shortfall.

As Minister, Kibaki moved swiftly to implement these proposals for a change of direction. He had an immediate reason for doing so: all the indicators which were available to the authorities suggested that the economy might have been suffering in 1969 from a depressed level of economic activity. Kibaki's first budget in the middle of 1970 therefore proposed a 17 per cent increase in the level of central government expenditures:

> I propose to take up the slack in the economy by expanding the Government development budget and to a lesser extent by also expanding the recurrent budget. . . .

> I have satisfied myself that the resources are available to support this expanded budget and that in the present circumstances of slackness in the economy there is an obligation on me to take the initiative in this matter. . . .

> This, I might add for the benefit of my fellow economists, does not mean that the budget is inflationary. It is designed to utilize human and capital resources that are now lying idle and to achieve an acceleration of the economy to a level it is quite capable of achieving without inflation.

The extra revenue required for this expanded budget was thus to be obtained, to a significant extent, by government borrowing from the monetary system. The writing of a new, Keynesian, conventional wisdom in the Kenya Treasury was now upon the wall.

The change in policy took some time to have any discernible effect upon the economy. Indeed, when the following year's budget was being prepared it appeared to the Treasury that the 1970 measures had been insufficient for their purpose, and that more were required. The 1971 budget therefore proposed a further large increase in expenditures, and an additional K.sh. 190 million of short term borrowing. In Kibaki's words,

> Once again . . . my budget is a budget for expansion. This is because there are still un-
> utilized resources in our economy and we want to put them to work.

4.32   Balance of Payments Crisis, 1971–72

It rapidly became evident however that the 1971 budget had been a serious mis-calculation. For the economic situation in Kenya in June 1971 was very different from what it had been one year earlier. In the first place, a large expansion of commercial bank credit to the private sector had been gathering pace since the beginning of 1970, and commercial bank liquidity had been falling steeply since the beginning of 1971. Second, although the Central Bank's reserves of foreign exchange were still comfortably above the minimum target level, they began to fall steeply from April 1971 onwards. Third, the cost of living indices in Nairobi, which were the government's main indicators of changes in the level of domestic prices generally, began at the same time to rise rather sharply at an annual rate of about 7 per cent. And finally, no subsequent evidence seemed to confirm the judgement that economic activity was at a low level in Kenya during 1971.

The initial steps to deal with the loss of foreign reserves were taken by the Central Bank, which had been aware for some time of the dangers of the new policy of short term borrowing, and which had at the end of 1969 imposed a $12\frac{1}{2}$ per cent statutory minimum liquid assets ratio upon the commercial banks as 'a credit tool in case of need'. Its first action to reverse the loss was the imposition in July 1971 of *selective* restrictions upon bank lending, aimed in particular at lending for hire purchase. But by the middle of November it was clear that this measure was having little impact upon the gathering foreign exchange crisis. The Bank then directed the commercial banks to place 5 per cent of the value of their deposit liabilities on special deposit – in effect, raising the statutory minimum liquidity ratio to $17\frac{1}{2}$ per cent.

This placed a binding constraint on lending by the majority of Kenya's commercial banks, and so brought the credit expansion to the private sector to an abrupt end. But it became apparent at once that the new credit restrictions were falling most severely upon small borrowers, and those whose security was less well established – which meant, in Kenya's circumstances, the *African* borrowers whom the government most wished to insulate from the restrictions.

Furthermore it was clear by the end of 1971 that restriction of bank credit to the private sector would not be sufficient by itself to prevent foreign reserves falling to the minimum target level, because the large credit expansion to the *public* sector which had been set in motion by the budgets of 1970–71 was still gaining momentum and could not be stopped. So aggregate monetary restriction was replaced, in January 1972, by direct restriction of imports: foreign exchange for transactions on current account was made subject to license, and quota limitations were imposed upon a wide variety of imports. At the same time, in an attempt to moderate the effects of these measures upon domestic prices, direct price controls were imposed upon all retail sales.

These measures were seen by the authorities as an essentially temporary response to an emergency situation, not as desirable instruments of economic management in the longer term. But before import restrictions could be relaxed it was necessary that the fiscal experiment which had led to the crisis should be reversed. This reversal was set in motion almost as thoroughly, and as swiftly, as the experiment itself. The budgets of 1972–73 thus made a concerted attempt to reimpose control upon the growth of government expenditure, and introduced several new sources of tax revenue (in particular, in the early months of 1973 a 10 per cent Sales Tax upon imported and locally manufactured articles). At the same time, the interests of the fiscal authorities began to shift perceptibly away from problems of short run stabilization and towards a long run reform of the tax system, designed to make government revenue more elastic and less dependent than it had been in the past upon the behaviour of imports.

4.33   Exchange Rate Policy

After November 1967 the new parity of the Kenya shilling remained fixed, and its effective exchange rate remained almost exactly constant until the middle of 1971. This interlude of calm was to be brought to an end, once again, by events outside Kenya's borders.

In August 1971 the pressures upon the relative values of the world's major trading currencies which had been increasingly apparent since 1967 came to a head. Concerned about a persistent loss of gold reserves, the USA suspended the convertibility of its dollar into gold, imposed a 10 per cent surcharge upon imports, and demanded a realignment of the exchange rates of the major trading currencies. For a time these currencies, including sterling, were allowed to 'float' against the dollar and inevitably most of them floated upwards.

Kenya at first maintained the parity of its shilling with sterling, which contributed to an appreciation of the shilling's effective exchange rate by about 1 per cent in the third quarter of 1971. But part of this appreciation was due to the fact that the Tanzanian authorities decided in August to maintain the value of their currency in terms of the dollar rather than sterling. The East African shillings were therefore no longer at par, and an important symbol of unity between the three countries of East Africa was in danger of disappearing. There followed urgent consultations between the authorities of the three countries, at which the

Tanzanian view prevailed: in October 1971 the Kenya and Uganda shillings rejoined that of Tanzania, fixed now in terms of the US dollar rather than sterling.

Whatever decision the Kenyan authorities had taken at this point about the peg to which the shilling was to be tied, it is clear with hindsight that the effective exchange rate of the shilling would have been subject to considerable change or fluctuation in the course of the next two years. In the event, the dollar peg which was chosen entailed a depreciation up to June 1972, when the pound sterling was floated; an appreciation from June to December 1972 as sterling floated downwards; a depreciation in the early months of 1973 when the dollar was devalued once again and the remaining trading currencies were allowed to float; and an appreciation in the second half of 1973 as the dollar recovered.

In 1973 however the East African countries were no longer prepared to remain passive in the face of such large and unplanned variations in the effective exchange rates of their currencies. In March and June 1973, when the relative value of the dollar was falling, the three East African shillings were revalued in small steps; and when the dollar recovered the East African shillings were devalued once again in January 1974. The effect of these changes was to offset some, but not all, of the instability to which the effective exchange rate of the Kenya shilling would otherwise have been subject, and to prevent it from departing too far in either direction from the level at which it had stood during the 1960s.

The practical target of Kenya's exchange rate policy was thus an approximately stable effective exchange rate for the shilling, in conjunction with the currencies of Tanzania and Uganda. Somewhat surprisingly perhaps, no public explanation or justification of this target was given. By the end of 1973 exchange rate policy in Kenya had become what aggregate fiscal and monetary policies had been eight years earlier – an instrument with a practical target, but no clearly defined role in controlling the behaviour of the national economy.

SUGGESTED READING

W. T. Newlyn and D. C. Rowan, *Money and Banking in British Colonial Africa* (Clarendon Press, 1954).
W. T. Newlyn, *Money in an African Context* (Oxford University Press, 1967).
International Bank for Reconstruction and Development, *The Economic Development of Kenya* (Johns Hopkins University Press, 1963).
International Monetary Fund, *Surveys of African Economies*, Vol. 2 (IMF, 1969).
P. Marlin (ed.), *Financial Aspects of Development in East Africa* (Munich: Weltforum-Verlag, 1970).
Central Bank of Kenya, *Money and Banking in Kenya* (CBK, 1972).

5 Modelling the Economy

Economics is a science of thinking in terms of models joined to the art of choosing models which are relevant to the contemporary world.

J. M. Keynes

5.1 CHOOSING A STARTING POINT

A national economy is an extremely complicated mechanism. One cannot hope to account for its behaviour exactly with any simplified model, let alone a model containing so few relationships that they can be counted upon the fingers of one hand. But it is necessary to try because the behaviour of an economy can only be understood to the extent that it can be *modelled* reasonably successfully.

In model-building there is always a conflict between simplicity on the one hand and, on the other, the exactness with which the model can be expected to reproduce the behaviour of a real economy. Other things being equal, simplicity is an important virtue; and for this reason it is desirable that a model-building exercise should begin with a very simple foundation. Chapter 2 outlined two alternative foundations. The obvious way to choose between them is to examine the extent to which the major implications of those two simple models correspond to what is known about the behaviour of the Kenyan economy.

5.11 *ODM's Implications and the Kenyan Experience*

ODM's main implication is that the level of economic activity is determined by the sum of 'autonomous expenditures' (investment, government spending and exports) according to a simple multiplier relationship – the value of the multiplier depending upon the economy's propensities to consume and to import. There is no presumption that this multiplier should remain constant over time. It may be altered, for example, by changes in tax rates; and it may tend to fall when autonomous expenditures are high and to rise when they are low, if the ratio between consumption and income falls as income rises. But there *is* presumption that a multiplier exists – in other words, that a fall in some component of autonomous expenditure will lead to an *amplified* fall in output.

So the first things that must be examined in the Kenyan context are the behaviour of economic activity, of those expenditures that ODM takes to be autonomous, and of the relationship over time between their respective fluctuations. To do this one must make use of the National Accounts – a set of statistics which is renowned (and not only in developing countries such as Kenya) for the fact that it is likely to contain rather wide margins of error. In Kenya official National Accounts have been published on a 'constant price' basis for each year since 1964.

These figures reveal a rapid growth in output and in all components of expenditure from 1964 onwards. Since our concern here is with economic *fluctuations*, the brief account which follows concentrates upon the deviations of these variables from their trend values rather than upon the absolute levels of the variables. The data to be discussed are presented in Table 5.1, and some important aspects are illustrated in Figure 5.1.

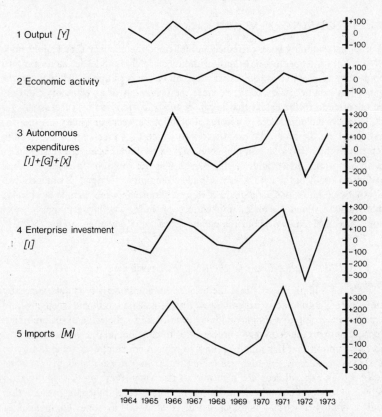

FIGURE 5.1 *Instability of Expenditures and Output in Kenya, 1964–73*

TABLE 5.1
Instability of Expenditures and Output in Kenya, 1964–73

Deviations from Trend* of:	Millions of Kenya Shillings (Constant 1964 Prices)						
	GDP at Factor Cost [Y]	GDP Excluding Agriculture	Enterprise Investment [I]	Government Spending [G]	Exports [X]	Autonomous Expenditures [I]+[G]+[X]	Imports [M]
1964	+24	− 37	− 48	− 24	+ 69	+ 5	− 84
1965	−88	− 9	−117	+ 16	− 49	−157	− 0
1966	+91	+ 44	+183	+ 4	+131	+298	+270
1967	−55	− 1	+112	+ 4	−133	− 44	− 12
1968	+41	+ 81	− 40	+ 11	−112	−170	−102
1969	+57	+ 3	− 72	+ 47	+ 32	− 18	−197
1970	−67	−105	+120	− 66	− 9	+ 33	− 61
1971	−14	+ 48	+272	+ 38	+ 0	+321	+390
1972	+14	− 24	−346	− 31	+ 84	−247	−154
1973	+72	+ 3	+191	−231	+ 62	+120	−314
Mean (Disregarding Sign)	52	35	150	47	68	141	158

Deviations from Trend* of:	Percentages of Trend Value						
	GDP at Factor Cost [Y]	GDP Excluding Agriculture	Enterprise Investment [I]	Government Spending [G]	Exports [X]	Autonomous Expenditures [I]+[G]+[X]	Imports [M]
1964	+0.5	−1.0	− 6.1	−2.1	+3.0	+0.1	− 4.0
1965	−1.7	−0.2	−13.2	+1.3	−2.0	−3.5	− 0.0
1966	+1.6	+1.0	+18.4	+0.3	+5.2	+6.1	+11.3
1967	−0.9	−0.3	+10.1	+0.2	−5.0	−0.8	− 0.5
1968	+0.6	+1.6	−3.2	+0.7	−4.1	−3.0	− 3.8
1969	+0.8	+0.6	−5.1	+2.5	+1.1	−0.3	− 6.9
1970	−0.9	−1.8	+ 7.6	−3.2	−0.3	+0.5	− 2.0
1971	−0.2	+0.7	+15.4	+1.6	+0.0	+4.4	+ 12.0
1972	+0.2	−0.3	−17.4	−1.2	+2.5	−3.2	− 4.4
1973	+0.8	+0.4	+ 8.6	−8.0	+1.8	+1.4	− 8.5
Mean (Disregarding Sign)	0.8	0.7	10.5	2.1	2.5	2.3	5.3

Source: Domestic expenditure data contained in Kenya's *Economic Surveys* and *Statistical Abstracts*, up to 1975.
* Trends fitted to observations up to 1972 only.

The main points that emerge from Table 5.1 may be summarized as follows:

1. In the years 1964–73 there is practically no instability of economic activity to be explained. Monetary GDP grew at a remarkably steady rate, deviating from its trend value, on average, by less than 1 per cent. When the agricultural sector is excluded (as we suggested in Chapter 1 that it should be) a similar picture emerges: according to this measure of economic activity, the degree of instability was indeed even smaller.

2. There is some suggestion in the Table that economic activity was low in the first two years of independence, rose to a peak in 1966–68, and then declined slightly until a further peak was reached in 1971. This pattern coincides quite

well with impressions formed by policy makers and observers in Kenya during the period. But the variations are extremely small, and almost certainly they lie well within the error margins of the underlying National Accounts figures.

3. By contrast, total autonomous expenditures fluctuated in a distinctly cyclical manner, with peaks in 1966 and 1971 and a trough in 1968. This total was substantially more unstable than economic activity, with a mean deviation from trend that was approximately four times as large in absolute terms. There was, therefore, no simple multiplier relationship in Kenya during the period: more or less systematic fluctuations in the value of

$$\left(\frac{1}{1 - c + m} \right)$$

offset almost all of the observed cyclical behaviour of autonomous expenditure.

4. Although enterprise investment amounted in absolute terms to less than one-quarter of total autonomous expenditures during the period, the deviations from trend of enterprise investment were very slightly larger than those of autonomous expenditures as a whole. The cylical behaviour of the latter is therefore largely accounted for by a pronounced investment cycle.

5. The systematic fluctuation in

$$\left(\frac{1}{1 - c + m} \right)$$

which has already been noted can be accounted for in large measure by variations in the propensity to import: imports followed a cyclical path almost identical to that of enterprise investment and total autonomous expenditures.

Points 4 and 5 in this list suggest a partial explanation for the absence of a multiplier relationship. For investment may well be expected to be more import-intensive than other components of expenditure in a developing country such as Kenya: so when investment rises and falls, domestic markets are insulated to some extent from these fluctuations. But a complete explanation cannot be provided along these lines. For Table 5.1 shows that in absolute terms the deviations from trend of imports were slightly *larger* than those of enterprise investment, and it is not plausible that the import coefficient of investment should be close to unity. Other factors must therefore have been at work.

One possibility suggested in the course of our discussion of model ODM in Chapter 2 is that the import coefficient might vary with changes in the rate of domestic inflation, arising from the changing pressure of autonomous and induced expenditures upon a fully employed economy – in other words, as a result of variations in an 'inflationary gap'. To test this hypothesis data are required on the domestic price level. Despite the familiar weaknesses of cost of living indices, the two Nairobi cost of living indices are probably the most reliable indicators of general price changes in Kenya during the years 1964–73, and were treated as such by the authorities. The annual rate of inflation suggested by these indices is illustrated in Figure 5.2. According to the indices, domestic inflation accelerated from zero in 1964 to an annual rate of about 4 per cent in 1966, declined to zero again in 1968, accelerated in 1970–71 to a peak of 8 per cent, and then subsided before a further acceleration in 1973.

This cyclical pattern matches quite closely the cycle of investment and autonomous expenditures, a fact which lends support to the hypothesis of a varying 'inflationary gap' throughout the period. (The evidence however has been presented in a rather casual manner. Strictly, of course, what should influence the import coefficient is the ratio between domestic and import prices, rather than the level of domestic prices alone; and this ratio coincides rather less closely with variations in the import coefficient.)

Enough has now been said, perhaps, to make the point that the economist who knows no macroeconomic model other than ODM is not compelled by the Kenyan evidence to lose faith in its usefulness. True, there is no trace of a multiplier in the Kenyan experience; but plausible explanations can be provided for this lapse, and a suitably modified version of ODM *can* be made consistent with the available evidence. This task is made easier by the fact that there is not a great deal of evidence against which the model can be tested, and easier still by the fact that such evidence as exists is not of the most reliable kind.

Average of the Nairobi cost of living indices : percentage increase over the previous year

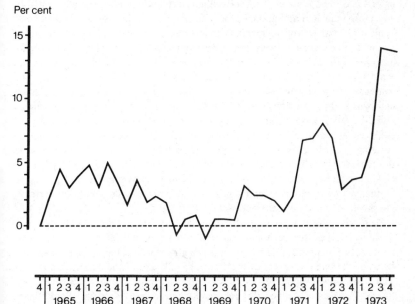

FIGURE 5.2 *Domestic Inflation in Kenya, 1964–73*

Nevertheless, it is quite clear that nobody who was not already familiar with ODM would dream of inventing anything similar to account for the behaviour of the Kenyan economy. The essential purpose of this model – to account for fluctuations in economic activity – is largely redundant in a study of Kenya in its first ten years of independence: there is simply no evidence of substantial fluctuations in this variable, so that ODM creates rather than solves a problem. And the fluctuations in prices and the balance of payments which *do* need explaining in the Kenyan context can be accounted for much more straightforwardly than by ODM.

5.12   MFF's Implications and the Kenyan Experience

The principal purpose of MFF, as originally developed in the 1950s by Polak, was to account for changes in the foreign reserves of an economy's monetary system. The model's implications are that foreign reserves will be influenced:

(i) positively, by changes in the rate of current account receipts plus net capital inflow on the balance of payments; and

(ii) negatively, in a one-to-one manner, by domestic credit expansion.

As Figures 5.3 and 5.4 illustrate, each of these implications on its own fits the Kenyan experience quite closely.

Balance of payments accounts have been prepared in Kenya on an annual basis since the middle of the 1960s. Such accounts are not generally felt to be any more reliable than national production and expenditure accounts. But some items in the balance of payments accounts can be calculated precisely in principle, and in practice are likely to be free from substantial errors. This is true for example of the balance of monetary movements, at least for a country which has a monetary system of its own, as Kenya has had since 1966. For a national central bank can tell by a glance at its own balance sheet, and those of the commercial banks which it controls, what the monetary system's net foreign assets are and how they have changed since the previous reckoning. These data are collected automatically in the normal accounting procedures of financial institutions – procedures which are enforced both by law and by the pressures of the market place. Of course, errors arise and there are practical problems of classification to be dealt with; but a part of what is shown in Figure 5.3 – namely, the balance of monetary movements from 1966 onwards – is almost certainly the most reliable data employed so far in this study.

And the same is true of *all* the data illustrated in Figure 5.4. The practical meaning of domestic credit expansion has already been explained, in the Kenyan context, in Chapter 2: it is measured straightforwardly from changes in specific items in the balance sheets of the Central Bank and of the commercial banks. The changes in foreign reserves shown in the Figure are changes in Kenya's *total* foreign reserves as defined throughout the period by the Central Bank. These reserves consisted predominantly of foreign assets held by the Bank itself, but included also the net foreign assets of the commercial banks, Kenya's gold tranche

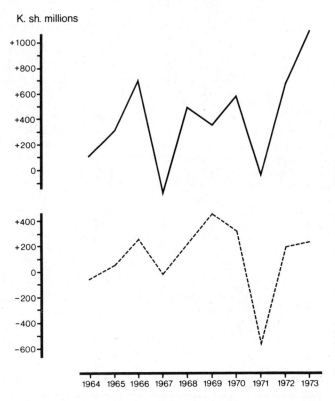

——— Change in *(X+F)* over previous year
--- Balance met by monetary movements

K. sh. millions

FIGURE 5.3 *Annual changes in Foreign Receipts and Monetary Movements in Kenya,
1964–73*

in the IMF, its share of some assets held by what was left of the East African
Currency Board, and a small stock of foreign assets held directly by the
government.

Therefore we are dealing at last with reasonably firm data, in reasonable
quantities; and it appears in Figures 5.3 and 5.4 to have behaved in a manner
that is consistent with MFF. It seems appropriate, then, to use MFF as a starting
point for a model of the Kenyan economy.

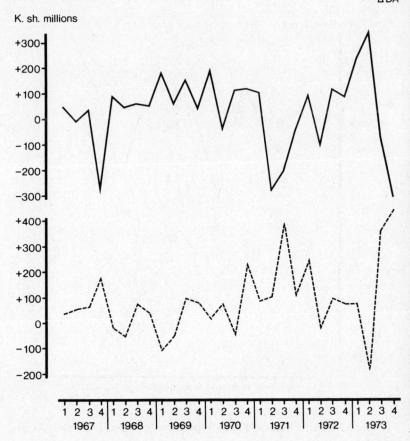

FIGURE 5.4 *Quarterly changes in Domestic Credit and Kenya's Foreign Reserves, 1967–73*

5.2   A SIMPLE QUARTERLY MODEL OF THE KENYAN ECONOMY (KEN)

KEN 1: $Y = A + X - M.$

KEN 2: $MO + SA = -900 + 1.7Y.$

KEN 3: $M = 100 + 0.4A.$

KEN 4: $\Delta(MO + SA) = \Delta FR - V + \Delta(DA - SA).$

KEN 5: $\Delta FR = X - M + F + V.$

5.21 *The Meaning of the Equations*

Equations KEN 1 to KEN 5 describe the relationships between a set of macroeconomic variables in particular periods of time. The time period is one-quarter of a calendar year; the variables are measured in millions of Kenya shillings.

KEN 1: $$Y = A + X - M.$$

This equation corresponds to MFF 1. Y is monetary GDP at current market prices, as shown in Kenya's National Accounts. X and M are gross current account inflows and outflows, as shown in the balance of payments accounts. Since the definition of X and M is not the same in the balance of payments and production and expenditure accounts, A has no exact counterpart in Kenya's official statistics, though it is the same in concept as what is there termed 'Resources Available for Domestic Investment and Consumption'.

KEN 2: $$MO + SA = -900 + 1.7Y.$$

This is a linear 'demand for money' function, very similar to MFF 2. MO is Kenya's money stock, as defined by the Kenyan authorities. This is a rather broad definition, comprising cash held by the non-bank private sector, private sector time and savings deposits with the commercial banks, and the deposits of the Post Office Savings Bank. SA is a crude seasonal adjustment factor, which will be explained when it reappears in equation KEN 4.

KEN 2 asserts that the demand for money rises faster than income, in a simple linear manner. One possible interpretation of this is that money is a 'luxury' good, with an income-elasticity of demand that is greater than unity. It seems probable, however, that a rather more complicated explanation is more appropriate here. Since 1967 the Kenyan authorities have taken progressive steps to 'Kenyanize' the private sector of the economy, by restricting the access of non-citizens to employment and to licences to trade. These steps have led to a steady emigration of a relatively wealthy group of non-citizens. But because of exchange control, such emigrants cannot immediately transfer their financial assets: these must be held for a time in Kenya, either in the form of medium term securities which the government sells specifically to satisfy this 'demand', or in the form of blocked accounts with the commercial banks. This means that the government can exert a direct influence upon MO, either by varying the rate of Kenyanization, or by varying its sales of privileged medium term securities to the holders of blocked accounts. Since the level of these accounts is not published, it is not possible to say in what way this influence has been used; but it is a reasonable guess that a significant part of the increase in MO in Kenya between 1966 and 1973 took the form of an increase in blocked account holdings. The parameters of KEN 2 may therefore reflect, to some extent, the discretionary behaviour of government, as well as that of the money-holding public.

KEN 3: $$M = 100 + 0.4A.$$

This is an import function very similar to MFF 3. Imports are, however, now said to depend upon domestic absorption rather than income. The assumption which is implicit here (as may be seen from footnote 5* in Chapter 2) is that the import coefficient of Kenya's exports is zero. This is certainly not true in practice, for about one-quarter of Kenya's visible exports consist of manufactured goods, many of them having a large import component. The equation is therefore to be regarded as a 'working exaggeration'.

The equation says that imports rise more slowly than absorption. Almost certainly, this reflects two rather different relationships – first, a short run relationship between M and A which might well be approximately proportional; and second, a long run tendency for the ratio of M to A to decline over time as the economy grows and new import-substituting industries develop. In practice, the data which is available in Kenya does not permit these separate relationships to be distinguished with confidence, and KEN 3 will be used as if it is a relationship which is stable in both the long run and the short.

KEN 4: $\Delta(MO + SA) = \Delta FR - V + \Delta(DA - SA).$

This equation is identical to MFF 4, apart from the subtraction of a new variable V from the asset side of the equation, and the fact that MO and DA are both adjusted, in opposite directions, by the seasonal adjustment factor SA. The new variable V will be discussed at a later stage, but this is a convenient point at which to explain SA.

As we showed in Chapter 2, the definition of ΔDA includes the change in the net indebtedness of the public sector to the banking system. But this variable, in Kenya as in most other countries, is subject to pronounced seasonal fluctuations because of the tendency for tax payments to be bunched at the end of each fiscal year. It is desirable to allow for this irregularity by introducing a seasonal adjustment. But if this is done in one part of an equation which is based upon an accounting identity, it is necessary that an offsetting adjustment should be introduced elsewhere in the equation. In essence, the assumption that has been made is that the private sector builds up its money balances in the first half of the fiscal year, with a view to making tax payments in the second half. SA takes the following values in successive quarters of each calendar year:

Q.1: −17.02; Q.2: −58.10; Q.3: +35.48; Q.4: +39.64.

KEN 5: $\Delta FR = X - M + F + V$

This is the same as MFF 5, apart from the appearance of the new variable V, which now requires an explanation.

In the world of the late 1960s and 1970s it is necessary to recognize that a country's foreign reserves, expressed in terms of domestic currency, can vary even though the value of $(X - M + F)$ is zero, as a result of two important influences. The first of these was the distribution of Special Drawing Rights (SDR) by the IMF, and the second is any revaluation of an existing stock of foreign assets, to take account of changes in the exchange rate. The value of V in each quarter is therefore the sum of SDR allocations, and revaluations of its foreign assets by the Central Bank of Kenya.

When the Central Bank gains or loses foreign assets in this way, it does not simultaneously gain or lose a domestic liability which is counted as money. Instead, it creates or cancels a non-monetary 'liability' of a notional kind in order to preserve the accounting identity between assets and liabilities. And this is why V must appear, not only in KEN 5, but in KEN 4 as well.

5.22 *The Exogenous Variables*

For the present, the four variables ΔDA, V, X and F are treated as exogenous, and the remaining variables of the model as endogenously determined.

Quarterly series for ΔDA and V have been obtained directly from published sources. But Kenya's balance of payments statistics are published only on an annual basis, and to obtain a quarterly series for X and F it has been necessary to improvise; the particular assumption that has been made is that the distribution of X and F in each calendar year from 1967 to 1973 was the same as that of exports, as recorded in Kenya's visible trade statistics. The resulting quarterly estimates are contained in Table 5.2 at the end of this chapter.

In addition, the model requires initial values for the two endogenous 'stock' variables, MO and FR. For this purpose the actual values of these variables at the end of 1966 have been taken:

KEN 6: $MO_{1966.4} = 1805.44,$

KEN 7: $FR_{1966.4} = 841.28.$

5.23 *The Derivation of the Parameters*

The parameters which appear in the only two behavioural equations of the model so far, KEN 2 and KEN 3, are clearly rather crude. They were originally derived in a rough trial-and-error manner, as follows. First, estimates of the parameters were obtained by plotting MO against Y, and M against A, on an annual basis. Then, the resulting equations were combined with the remaining equations of the model and data for the exogenous variables, to generate 'predictions' of the endogenous variables FR, MO and Y. It was found that these predictions departed consistently from the actual values of the endogenous variables. The parameters were then adjusted gradually in an *ad hoc* manner until the predicted variables seemed on inspection to be tolerably close to their actual values.

One advantage of this method of estimating the parameters is that it does not require the use of an electronic computer. Against this must be set the possible disadvantage, that it is likely to arouse some suspicion in those readers who are accustomed to more formal estimation procedures.

An obvious alternative would be to obtain direct estimates of the parameters by regressing MO on Y, and M on A (or preferably on $(A - M)$, since M is a component of A and will therefore necessarily be correlated with it). However such an approach leads to estimates which in practice have been found to be inferior to those of model KEN. And there are several good reasons why the use of ordinary least squares (OLS) methods to estimate these parameters should not be expected to yield good results.

In the first place, 'actual' figures for Y, M and A can be obtained only on an annual basis, so that there are only seven observations from which to derive OLS estimates. Furthermore, all three of these series are probably subject to substantial errors of observation, so that one of the fundamental assumptions of OLS estimation – namely, that errors of observation are present only in the dependent variable – will be violated.

Second, in model KEN the two behavioural equations are not independent: they are part of a system. And when this system is examined as a whole, it is found that its parameters are not properly 'identified'. In these circumstances OLS is likely to give biased estimates. Other estimating techniques are available which can eliminate this bias, on various assumptions; but none of the methods tried so far gives more satisfactory estimates than the ones that were originally obtained by simple trial and error, in the manner described above.

Third, model KEN describes an economy in a process of adjustment, not in a state of equilibrium. In formal terms, the systems of equations contains a lagged endogenous variable, and this is yet another potential source of bias in OLS estimates.

The reader may well begin to feel at this point that a model based upon MFF suffers from some serious practical disadvantages which would not be present in a model based upon ODM. But such a conclusion would be entirely wrong. For a model based upon ODM would encounter similar data problems; and it would avoid the problem raised by the presence of a lagged endogenous variable only because ODM portrays an economy that is in equilibrium all the time. In an empirical study such a hypothesis would be clearly absurd. The fact of the matter is that the practical problems which have been touched upon in this section are unavoidable in the empirical application of *any* macroeconomic model, irrespective of how simple or complex the model may appear.

5.24   *The Results*

Of the time series whose behaviour is reproduced by the model, three are variables whose *actual* behaviour in the years 1967–73 is shown in Kenya's official statistics: *FR, MO* and *Y*. The most important test of the model is its ability to explain the behaviour of the first of these. The quarterly pattern of Kenya's foreign reserves, as it was in fact and as reproduced by model KEN, is illustrated in Figure 5.5.

It is clear from this diagram that KEN reproduces the distinctive pattern of *FR* behaviour in Kenya reasonably closely. KEN successfully 'predicts' the sharp fall in *FR* at the end of 1967, the steady and rapid increase from 1968 until the end of 1970, the fall during 1971 and the first half of 1972, the sharp recovery up to the middle of 1973 and the fall during the second half of the year.

Its most obvious weakness is that it predicts a reserve loss in 1971–72 beginning one quarter earlier, lasting one quarter longer, and generally being rather less dramatic than it was in practice. But the departures of KEN's predictions from actual *FR* behaviour are nowhere very large. The predictions are as close as could reasonably be hoped for.

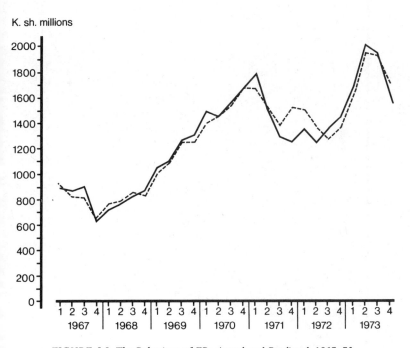

FIGURE 5.5 *The Behaviour of FR: Actual and Predicted, 1967–73*

The second variable of some interest which KEN predicts is *MO*: actual and predicted values of this variable are illustrated in Figure 5.6. As this diagram shows, Kenya's money stock grew between 1967 and 1973 remarkably steadily, at a gradually increasing rate. This is a simple pattern, but it is one that KEN reproduces almost exactly. (It should perhaps be noted here that Figure 5.6 may look rather more impressive on its own than it really is. For the three variables ΔDA, ΔFR and ΔMO are linked together in principle in an identity. So long as one's practical measures of these three variables do not seriously violate the terms of the identity, reasonably close predictions of *FR* such as those shown in Figure 5.5 necessarily imply good predictions of *MO*, and conversely. Figure 5.6

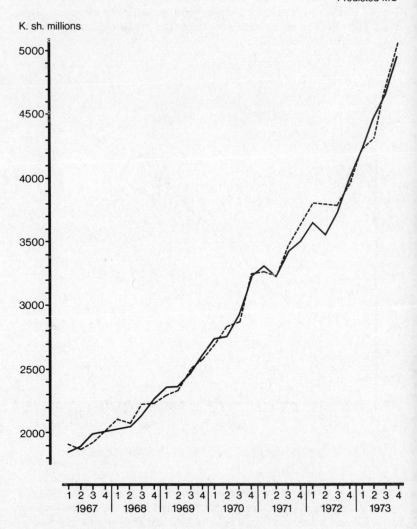

FIGURE 5.6 *The Behaviour of MO: Actual and Predicted, 1967–73*

is nevertheless important, because it shows that money stock behaviour in Kenya can be successfully explained by a model such as KEN which treats the money stock as an endogenous variable which is of little interest in its own right.)

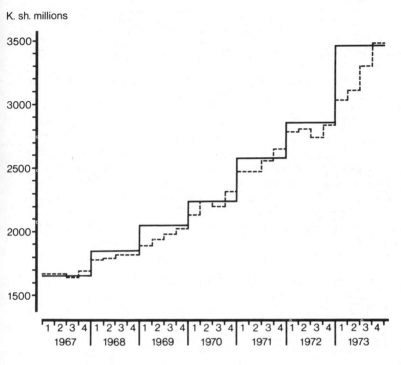

FIGURE 5.7 *The Behaviour of Y: Actual and Predicted, 1967–73*

Finally, KEN's quarterly predictions of Y are compared with the actual values of this variable (on an annual basis, but at a quarterly rate) in Figure 5.7. As has been noted, the 'actual' values of Y probably have a rather wide margin of error. Furthermore this series is periodically revised, so that in constructing a model to reproduce its behaviour one is chasing a moving target. However it may be seen in Figure 5.7 that nominal income in Kenya, like the money stock, grew in the years 1967–73 at a fairly steadily increasing rate; and it is this pattern, which has been preserved in all revisions of the official statistics, that KEN reproduces.

5.25   *An Extension of the Model: Prices and Economic Activity*

Chapter 2 showed that it is a straightforward matter to extend model MFF to provide an explanation of domestic price level behaviour by adding an assumption about the behaviour of output. In Section 5.11 of the present chapter it has been shown that output in Kenya grew very steadily during the first ten years of the country's independence, despite considerable fluctuations in autonomous expenditures; and it is reasonable to interpret this finding as evidence that economic activity was maintained during the period close to its full employment level. So an obvious extension of model KEN is suggested: to add some further equations similar to MFF 6 to MFF 9, to calculate KEN's 'equilibrium' level of domestic prices for each quarter, and to compare this predicted variable with such evidence as there is about the actual behaviour of prices in Kenya during the period.

The additional behavioural equation, which corresponds to MFF 6, is as follows:

KEN 8: $[Y]_t = 1450(1.01816)^t$

where 1.01816 is the actual trend growth rate, on a quarterly basis, of Kenya's monetary GDP at factor cost measured at constant 1964 prices; and 1450 is a value for this variable in the base period (the fourth quarter of 1966), chosen rather roughly in such a way as to produce an index of the equilibrium level of domestic prices P_A that is close to the average value of the two Nairobi cost of living indices in this base period.

The other equations that are necessary correspond exactly to MFF 7 to MFF 9:

KEN 9: $P_A = \dfrac{A}{[Y] - [X] + [M]}$,

KEN 10: $X = \dfrac{[X] \cdot P_X}{R}$,

KEN 11: $M = \dfrac{[M] \cdot P_M}{R}$.

To generate predictions of the behaviour of the domestic price level P_A, quarterly indices are now required for the three new exogenous variables P_X and P_M (the foreign currency prices of Kenya's exports and imports respectively) and R (the effective exchange rate of the Kenya shilling). These can be derived, albeit rather roughly, from official data: the estimates which result are shown in Table 5.2 at the end of the chapter. On the basis of these estimates, KEN's equations produce quarterly predictions of P_A. These predictions are compared in Figure 5.8 with the behaviour of the Nairobi cost of living indices in the period 1967–73.

The first point to be made about this diagram is that KEN's equilibrium price level P_A behaves rather erratically, with some trace in the late 1960s of seasonal fluctuation. The second point is that the sharp rise in KEN's predicted P_A from the end of 1970 to the beginning of 1972 was followed, only with a very pronounced lag, by the Nairobi cost of living indices. It is quite clear that if KEN's predictions are regarded as predictions of *actual* price behaviour, they are not very good.

But Figure 5.8 is nevertheless wholly consistent with the view that P_A, as predicted by KEN, was an equilibrium price level towards which actual prices

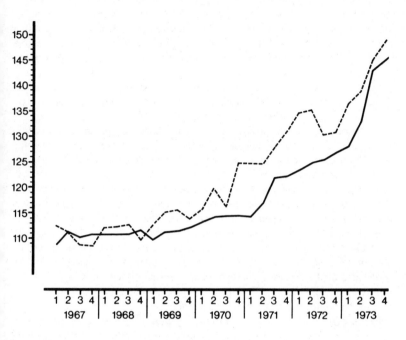

——— Actual, average of the Nairobi
cost of living indices (1964 = 100)
--- Predicted P_A

FIGURE 5.8 *The Behaviour of Domestic Prices: The Nairobi Cost of Living Indices and Predicted P_A, 1967–73*

were moving throughout the period. The greater instability of P_A than of observed prices can easily be explained by an element of 'stickiness' in aggregate price behaviour in the real world (particularly as measured by cost of living indices). And the temporary lag of actual prices behind predicted prices during 1971 can easily be accounted for by the suggestion put forward in Section 5.11 that economic activity in Kenya was slightly below trend in 1969–70, but rose to a peak in 1971: to the extent that a rise in the *equilibrium* level of domestic prices has a temporary effect in the first instance upon the level of economic activity, the resulting rise in *actual* prices is delayed. So if one allows for an element of price inflexibility in the Kenyan economy, model KEN can account fairly straightforwardly for what is roughly known about the behaviour both of domestic prices and of economic activity in Kenya in the late 1960s and early 1970s.

5.3   FURTHER DEVELOPMENT OF THE MODEL

5.31   *The Stability of the Demand for Money*

In model KEN the 'demand for money' is a linear function of nominal income, and nothing else. This simple assumption clearly fits the Kenyan experience of the period 1967–73. But we have already added one qualification, by suggesting in Section 5.21 that the 'demand for money' may have been directly influenced, in practice, by some features of government policy. It is now necessary to extend this qualification.

In the first place, as suggested in Chapter 4, before exchange control was introduced in 1965 deliberate variations in the level of domestic interest rates relative to those elsewhere had an important effect upon the demand for domestic money balances, and a corresponding effect upon private sector capital movements. Without a reasonably watertight system of exchange control, the demand for domestic money balances in Kenya would undoubtedly be sensitive to such interest rate differentials.

Second, there are good theoretical reasons for expecting the demand for nominal money balances to vary not only with the level of interest rates, but also with variations in the expected rate of domestic inflation. With a given structure of nominal interest rates, inflation imposes a penalty upon all those who hold wealth in the form of financial assets including money, and so should lead to an attempt to substitute real assets for financial ones. It was therefore to be expected that the domestic inflation which became evident in Kenya in 1971, and more strongly from 1973 onwards, should eventually lead to a downward shift in the desired ratio of money to income.

In principle it is straightforward to modify model KEN so as to incorporate such relationships. The result is simple: a downward shift in the demand for MO has exactly the same effect upon all of KEN's endogenously determined variables, except of course MO itself, as an equivalent credit expansion ΔDA. Such relationships have not been included in model KEN, not because they are likely to be unimportant, but because there is at present insufficient evidence in Kenya to enable one to make a reasonable estimate of their magnitude and timing.

5.32   *The Effect of Import Restrictions*

Severe import restrictions were imposed in Kenya in January 1972, and they remained in force until a gradual relaxation was commenced in the middle of 1973. It is generally supposed that such restrictions should affect an economy's import function, and that their likely impact should be analysed accordingly. But KEN has succeeded in 'explaining' most of the behaviour of the important macroeconomic variables in Kenya, and in particular that of foreign reserves, without taking any effect of this kind into account. This may well seem surprising.

A fairly straightforward explanation can be given however. On the whole, it seems that the initial response of firms to the restriction of their ability to import was to draw upon their existing stocks of intermediate and finished goods. This reduced their need for short term finance from the banks; and it also reduced in volume the kind of security against which the banks were accustomed to grant advances. As a result, no bank credit expansion to the private sector took place between the beginning of 1972 and the middle of 1973. As deposits continued to rise, the ratio of bank advances to deposits therefore fell. When import restrictions began to be relaxed, however, this excess liquidity was rapidly used up in a renewed credit expansion. Hence, import restrictions did indeed restrict imports. But they did so for the most part indirectly, through their effect upon bank credit. A *direct* effect upon the import function might indeed become evident if import controls were to remain in force for a long period of time, but there is no clear evidence of such an effect in Kenya during the period covered by this study.

5.33 *The Credit Cycle in Kenya*

The interpretation of the effect of import controls given in the last section relies upon a fairly stable relationship between the level of bank advances to the private sector on the one hand, and the level of business stocks on the other. This relationship was in fact a close one in Kenya, not just in the years 1972–73, but throughout the whole period covered by this study. The investment cycle which was described in Section 5.11 was, to a large extent, a *stockbuilding* cycle; and this was matched, in turn, by a cycle in the behaviour of bank credit to the private sector.

But private sector deposits with the commercial banks rose closely in step with the money stock as a whole, which grew in a fairly stable manner. As a result, the cyclical pattern of bank credit expansion to the private sector was reflected in a cyclical variation in the ratio of private sector deposits to private sector advances. Furthermore, since public sector deposits with and advances from the commercial banks remained relatively small and the balance between them roughly stable, the ratio of *all* commercial bank advances to deposits – that is, roughly, the inverse of what is taken in Kenya to be the 'liquidity ratio' of the commercial banks – fluctuated in a similar cyclical manner. This point is illustrated in Figure 5.9.

Now, there is a natural tendency for economists to seek mechanical explanations for the kind of cyclical patterns illustrated in this diagram – a sort of 'tide in the affairs of men'. But most contemporary observers of the Kenyan economy were content with explanations of an *ad hoc* kind, along something like the following lines.

The banks were judged to be in an approximately 'fully loaned up' position in the early part of 1967; they allowed their liquidity to fall temporarily early in 1968 in response to emergency demands for credit and withdrawals of deposits following the devaluation of sterling; their liquidity then rose substantially because of a depressed demand for credit following the introduction of

Kenyanization measures in 1968 and political uncertainties in 1969; it fell steeply towards a more normal level as stockbuilding recovered in 1970 and 1971; but the fall was arrested at the end of 1971 by the Central Bank's credit restrictions, and then reversed by the imposition of import restrictions. It is possible of course that there is more to the story than this; but it does not appear that anything more is required to explain the cycle of bank credit and bank liquidity in Kenya in the period covered by this study.

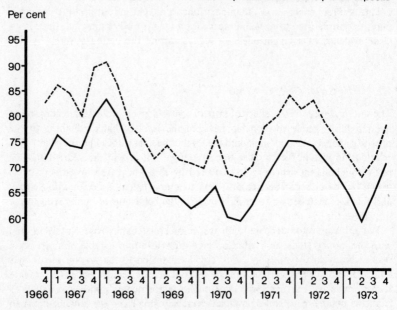

FIGURE 5.9 *Ratio of Commercial Banks' Advances to Deposits and Ratio of Private Advances to Deposits, 1966–73*

5.34 Some Further Equations

The matters discussed in the previous few sections suggest that it would be useful to develop the model a little further, to incorporate the commercial banks and their balance sheet separately. This is a straightforward matter. First, a further behavioural equation is required to explain the level of commercial bank deposits from the private sector. An equation which reproduces the close linear relationship between private deposits (PD) and the money stock in Kenya between 1966 and 1973 is:

KEN 12: $PD = -145 + 0.8MO.$

Second, private deposits are related to commercial bank lending to the private sector (DA_P) in the balance sheet ratio:

KEN 13: $$DA_P = b \cdot PD.$$

(As we have seen, b fluctuated in a cyclical manner in Kenya during the period; but a rough estimate of b with the banks in a 'fully loaned up' position would be about 0.83.)

Third, by definition, *total* domestic credit by the monetary system consists of credit to the public sector on the one hand (DA_G), and the private sector on the other; and so

KEN 14: $$\Delta DA \cong \Delta DA_G + \Delta DA_P.$$

In the same spirit, it will be useful for us to distinguish between foreign capital flows to the public and private sectors:

KEN 15: $$F \equiv F_G + F_P.$$

Finally, an initial value is required for bank lending to the private sector at the end of 1966:

KEN 16: $$DA_{P(1966.4)} = 1071.88.$$

With the exception of one final equation to be introduced in the next chapter, this completes our model of the Kenyan economy.

5.4 CONCLUSION

This chapter has developed a simple model to account for the behaviour of the balance of payments, the level of prices, and the level of economic activity in Kenya. The model contains three important behavioural equations – a 'demand for money' function (KEN 2), an import function (KEN 3), and a crude assumption about the behaviour of economic activity (KEN 8, which may be qualified informally to allow for an element of price inflexibility). And the model contains eight main exogenous variables, which may be grouped as follows:

(1) P_X and P_M, which are determined on world markets;
(2) $[X]$, which may be regarded in the short run as given;
(3) F_P and ΔDA_P (or b), which may be influenced by the authorities but not, perhaps, in a simple and direct manner; and
(4) F_G, ΔDA_G and R, which are instruments of stabilization policy.

The model provides an account of how the Kenyan economy behaved in the years 1967–73 – an account which is reasonably consistent with its actual behaviour. But it also tells a story about how the economy was influenced by government policy, and how it would have behaved had this policy been different. Some important parts of this story will be examined in the next chapter.

TABLE 5.2
Exogenous Variables of Model KEN, 1967–73

Year and Quarter	[X]*	[F]*	[F_P]*	ΔDA†	ΔDA_P†	V†	R‡	P_X§	P_M§
1967 1	716.98	119.53	68.83	− 41.02	74.48	−	1.021	1.033	1.055
2	652.34	105.76	60.20	14.58	38.14	−	1.033	1.038	1.060
3	685.78	111.56	63.50	68.12	5.30	− 71.56	1.033	1.048	1.075
4	670.08	113.53	61.47	59.08	116.84	+ 0.08	1.086	1.063	1.093
1968 1	767.18	187.14	89.44	− 55.52	38.18	−	1.084	1.075	1.108
2	740.77	175.69	84.28	− 7.96	43.60	−	1.080	1.080	1.120
3	777.74	183.75	88.06	117.00	41.28	−	1.081	1.083	1.128
4	707.47	171.24	82.22	13.46	25.10	−	1.079	1.080	1.133
1969 1	847.57	188.89	100.10	− 91.36	19.54	−	1.083	1.073	1.133
2	843.01	181.40	96.22	− 85.92	44.96	−	1.082	1.070	1.135
3	855.06	182.86	97.00	70.52	20.78	+ 95.58	1.082	1.070	1.138
4	800.80	178.30	94.67	31.94	45.50	−	1.081	1.085	1.140
1970 1	844.47	220.33	85.56	− 53.50	70.64	+ 38.40	1.082	1.115	1.143
2	864.27	224.11	87.35	55.06	129.66	−	1.078	1.145	1.150
3	855.98	223.48	87.35	15.26	63.62	−	1.075	1.160	1.160
4	931.59	250.28	97.73	92.48	134.28	−	1.076	1.163	1.180
1971 1	867.37	170.72	59.78	− 41.96	126.18	+ 43.84	1.082	1.163	1.205
2	852.57	162.76	57.10	− 70.96	−171.04	−	1.080	1.165	1.230
3	896.06	170.73	59.29	197.00	183.04	−	1.091	1.170	1.255
4	931.85	183.86	67.83	0.34	109.34	+ 84.74	1.027	1.180	1.285
1972 1	855.39	230.89	89.42	221.32	20.38	+ 47.68	1.013	1.200	1.315
2	939.31	249.48	93.84	− 23.68	1.30	−145.14	1.043	1.220	1.345
3	850.76	231.01	86.48	144.60	− 47.80	−	1.048	1.255	1.380
4	921.81	266.23	98.26	7.38	42.96	−	1.063	1.300	1.420
1973 1	925.73	329.18	191.18	62.88	29.58	+ 42.76	1.030	1.350	1.465
2	932.43	333.31	200.47	−248.46	67.58	+ 71.02	0.993	1.400	1.510
3	903.32	332.38	192.73	122.30	240.74	− 57.32	1.030	1.450	1.570
4	861.09	338.79	189.63	17.94	422.44	− 93.72	1.067	1.510	1.620

NOTES:
* Quarterly values of X and F have been derived from Kenya's balance of payments and visible trade accounts in the manner explained in the text. These figures have then been deflated by R and P_x, as appropriate, to derive figures for [X] and [F].
† Figures obtained straightforwardly from CBK *Annual Reports*. In the case of V, additional unpublished information provided by the CBK about its revaluations has been used to derive the figures for 1972 and 1973.
‡ A rather crude effective exchange rate index derived from currency values contained in IMF, *International Financial Statistics*. The weights used are the share of each country in Kenya's visible trade in the years 1965–71.
§ Kenya's official import and export price indices have been deflated by the average value of R during each year to obtain an annual value for P_M and P_x. These

6 Some Lessons from the Model

In real life the right thing never happens at the right place at the right time: it is the business of the historian to remedy this mistake.

Mark Twain

6.1 INTRODUCTION

This chapter has two aims. The first is to explore the ways in which the new departures in stabilization policy which were introduced in the early 1970s affected the Kenyan economy, using the model developed in Chapter 5. The second is more general – to examine how, according to this model, the economy could in principle have been managed with available instruments of policy in such a way as to maintain stability in the balance of payments, domestic prices and economic activity.

Our procedure is to compare model KEN's version of what actually happened, given the ways in which those instruments of policy which appear among its exogenous variables were used, with its account of what would have happened had those instruments been used differently. This procedure involves using KEN as a simple simulation model, to generate predictions on the basis of a succession of different assumptions about the exogenous variables. The particular assumptions made in the various simulations that are reported in this chapter are summarized in Table 6.1.

6.2 THE FISCAL EXPERIMENT, 1970–73

6.21 *The Impact of the Fiscal Experiment upon KEN's Exogenous Variables*

Perhaps the most striking measure of the change in fiscal policy at the beginning of the 1970s was a steep rise in the ratio of central government expenditures to monetary GDP at current market prices, from a plateau at about 30 per cent up to the fiscal year 1968–69 to 38 per cent in 1970–71. Part of this increase was due simply to the transfer of responsibility for a number of services from local

TABLE 6.1
Assumptions made in the Simulations

	P_X, P_M	$[X]$	$[F]$	F_G	F_P	$\Delta(DA_G - SA)$	$\Delta DA_{|P}$	b	R	V	P_A
S1 (Chapter 5)	a	a	a	—	—	a	a	—	a	a	en
S2	a	a	a	—	—	a	a	—	a	=0	en
S3	a	a	a	—	—	=0	a	en	a	=0	en
S4	a	a	a	=84	a	=0	a	en	a	=0	en
S5	a	a	a	—	—	=0	a*	=0.83†	a	=0	en
S6	a	a	a	—	—	=0	—	=0.83	a	=0	en
S7	a	a	a	—	—	=0.01Y	—	=0.83	a	=0	en
S8	a	tr	tr	—	—	=0	—	=0.83	en‡	en§	=112.15
S9	a	tr	tr	—	—	=0.01Y	—	=0.83	en‡	en§	=112.15
S10	a	tr	tr	—	—	=0.01Y	—	=0.83	en¶	en§	en

NOTES:

a   'actual' value, shown in Table 5.2.

en   endogenous.

tr   trend value of a.

*   up to 1971.3 only.

†   from 1971.4 onwards.

‡   chosen in each period so as to maintain $P_A = 112.15$.

§   determined according to the equation $V = FR_{-1} \cdot \left(1 - \dfrac{R}{R_{-1}}\right)$.

¶   chosen in each period so as to maintain $X + F - M = 0$.

authorities to the central government in 1970, but most of it was a genuine increase in public sector expenditure as a whole and, as we showed in Chapter 4, it was a deliberate increase.

But the level of government expenditures as such does not appear among KEN's variables. In the model, government expenditures exert an influence upon foreign reserves, prices and the level of economic activity only to the extent that they are financed by bank credit and foreign borrowing. The effects of the fiscal experiment therefore flow in model KEN simply from the consequent changes in F_G and ΔDA_G.

In the first place, F_G rose from an annual level of about K.sh. 300 millions up to 1969, to about K.sh. 500 millions from 1970 to 1973. (The rise was not quite so abrupt as that of central government expenditure, and there was some fluctuation about these average figures.) In terms of its impact upon KEN's endogenous variables, a rise in F_G amounting to about K.sh. 50 millions in each quarter is relatively insignificant: in what follows the effect of changes in F_G will be described verbally rather than illustrated diagrammatically.

The second and much more important departure on the revenue side of the government accounts in the early 1970s was the commencement of substantial short term borrowing from the monetary system. The behaviour of DA_G on a seasonally adjusted basis between the end of 1966 and the end of 1973 is illustrated in Figure 6.1.

It is rather important to note the scale and the precise timing of the change that is shown in this diagram. Between 1966 and 1973 the total increase in DA_G was about K.sh. 480 millions. But this credit expansion was not a steady one: it was more than fully concentrated into a relatively short period between about the third quarter of 1971 and the first quarter of 1973. Although the decisions which led to this credit expansion were taken in the early months of 1970 (as was shown in Chapter 4) the impact of these decisions was delayed by an unexpectedly buoyant level of tax receipts and government long term borrowing on the Nairobi market during the boom of 1970–71. Indeed, it was not until the boom was ended in the last months of 1971 that the government *actually* began to borrow on a substantial scale from the monetary system.

The outcome of central government budgets in the early 1970s was therefore slightly different, at least in its timing, from what had been intended. But it is outcomes rather than intentions that matter in this chapter, for it is outcomes that appear as KEN's exogenous variables.

6.22 *The Fiscal Experiment, Prices and Economic Activity*

To investigate the effects of the fiscal experiment, three simulations will first be compared:

S2: in which all of KEN's exogenous variables (except V, which does not become relevant until the second half of this chapter) take their actual values;

S3: in which no government borrowing from the monetary system takes place apart from seasonal fluctuation, so that $\Delta(DA_G - SA)$ is zero in all quarters, but all other exogenous variables take their actual values; and

S4: in which F_G is restricted to its level in the year 1966 (namely 84 per quarter), $\Delta(DA_G - SA)$ is zero, but all other exogenous variables take their actual values.

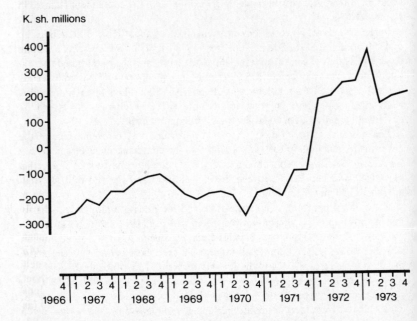

FIGURE 6.1 *Public Sector Indebtedness to the Monetary System, 1966–73 (seasonally adjusted)*.

S4 therefore shows what would have happened if the experiment had not taken place, on the very strong assumption that KEN's other exogenous variables were not affected, and on this same assumption the difference between the predictions of S4 and S2 measures the effect of the experiment.

The question that is to be answered in this section is the extent to which the experiment proved inflationary. Figure 6.2, which shows S2's predictions of the equilibrium domestic price level P_A as a percentage of those of S4, tells a straightforward story. Until the third quarter of 1970, actual changes in aggregate fiscal policy had no systematic influence upon P_A. Fiscal changes then raised P_A above the level at which it would otherwise have stood – by about 2 per cent throughout 1971; by 6 per cent from the beginning of 1972 to the beginning of 1973; and by 2 per cent for the remainder of 1973. Very roughly, the *permanent* 2 per cent step upwards at the end of 1970 was due to changes in government's foreign borrowing, whereas the additional *temporary* 4 per cent upward step during 1972 was due to borrowing from the banking system.

These arithmetical findings may now be interpreted in a more informal manner. Economic activity appears to have been at a relatively high level in 1971, and prices rose quite sharply. Figure 6.2 suggests that some part of this behaviour might be attributed to a higher level of government spending, financed by foreign borrowing. But the inflationary effect of this was rather small and it was confined to the end of 1970. The sharp and temporary rise in P_A at the beginning of 1972, on the other hand, came at a time when *actual* prices in Kenya were subject to administrative control, and were gradually catching up with their equilibrium levels. At most, it seems reasonable to suppose that the large credit expansion to the government during 1972 prevented economic activity from falling further than might otherwise have been the case: it did not affect actual prices.

The main conclusion that is suggested, therefore, is that the fiscal experiment had almost no direct effect upon the behaviour of prices in Kenya. In the seven year period 1967–73, when the Nairobi cost of living indices rose by 33 per cent and KEN's predicted equilibrium price level rose by 32 per cent, only two percentage points of the latter can be attributed to the change in fiscal policy in the early 1970s.

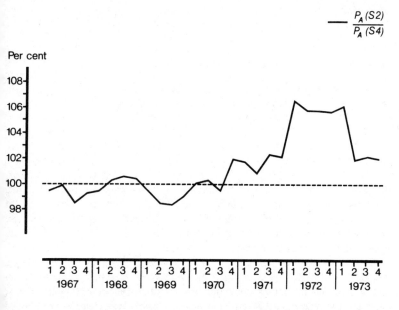

FIGURE 6.2 *The Impact of the Fiscal Experiment on P_A*

6.23   *The Fiscal Experiment and Foreign Reserves*

This negative conclusion should not come as a surprise. It may be recalled from Chapter 2 that in model MFF, credit expansion has only a temporary effect upon prices and economic activity, but a permanent effect upon the level of foreign reserves; and model KEN is simply an applied version of model MFF.

The effect of the 1972 credit expansion to the Kenya government does not immediately strike the eye when one examines the pattern of foreign reserve behaviour, because many other influences were at work at the same time. But it can be seen clearly if one compares KEN's predictions of foreign reserve behaviour given the credit expansion to the government that actually took place (S2), with its predictions of what would have happened without this credit expansion (S3). (In order to make the comparison as clear as possible, it is convenient to disregard the exogenous changes V and to concentrate attention upon the underlying pattern of *induced* foreign reserve changes. In practice V had an important effect upon Kenya's reserves in particular quarters, but its net effect in the years 1967–73 was to add only K.sh. 56 millions.)

The pattern of foreign reserve behaviour in KEN's simulations S2 and S3 is illustrated in Figure 6.3. This diagram shows that credit expansion to the government had very little effect upon the behaviour of foreign reserves up to the middle of 1971 – not surprisingly, since Figure 6.1 has shown that there was very little of it. But by the end of 1972, foreign reserves were almost K.sh. 500 millions lower than they would have been if no such credit expansion had taken place. And whereas the effect of this credit expansion upon prices and economic activity was temporary, its effect upon the reserves was permanent.

6.24   *The Need for Credit Restriction and Import Controls*

So far it has been assumed that the fiscal experiment had no effect upon any of KEN's exogenous variables apart from F_G and ΔDA_G. But in at least one important respect, this assumption is an implausible one: ΔDA_P would almost certainly have behaved rather differently if the experiment had not been undertaken.

In the first place, it is possible that some part of the bank credit expansion to the private sector which actually took place during 1971 was stimulated by the 2 per cent rise in the equilibrium price level in the previous year that has been attributed to an increase in the rate of government's external borrowing. Second, and much more important, it is quite certain that this credit expansion would not have collapsed dramatically during 1972 in the absence of import controls, and the need for those controls – to the extent that they were indeed needed – arose solely from the fiscal experiment.

Credit restrictions and import controls were introduced in 1971–72 in response to a rapid loss of foreign reserves, which threatened to reduce them below the Central Bank's minimum target level. The measures were almost successful in defending this target: in practice, Kenya's foreign reserves dipped only briefly below the target level, and by a small amount, in the middle of 1972.

But if no credit expansion to the government had taken place, there would have been very little risk of their doing so.

For according to KEN's simulation S3, the commercial banks' private advances: deposits ratio b would have risen by the third quarter of 1971 above 83 per cent, the level which we have suggested represented an approximately 'fully loaded up' position for the commercial banks. The banks would then have begun to take steps of their own accord to moderate their credit expansion; and in doing so they would automatically have brought the loss of foreign reserves to an end before the Central Bank's minimum reserve target was threatened. (Of course, it is possible that the banks would have allowed b to rise temporarily above 83 per cent, as they had done in 1968 after the devaluation of sterling, and were to do again in 1974–75 in the wake of the oil crisis; but it is wholly unreasonable to suppose that they would have allowed it to rise continuously, for this would have been possible only if they had been able and willing to borrow increasing amounts from foreign banks.)

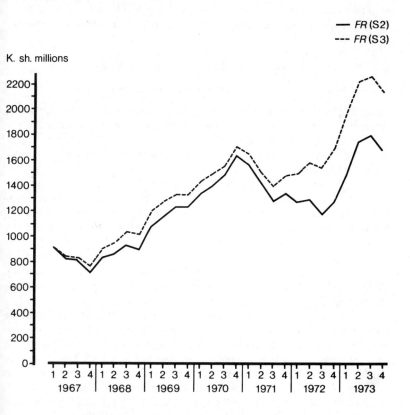

FIGURE 6.3 *The Impact of the Fiscal Experiment on FR*

This argument suggests a further arithmetical exercise for KEN – namely to reproduce the behaviour of foreign reserves during the 1970s as it would have been if no credit expansion to the government had taken place, and if b had been kept at 83 per cent from the end of 1971 onwards; and to compare this with the way in which the Central Bank's minimum target would have behaved. To perform this exercise one final equation is required to explain the behaviour of the reserve target. An equation which reproduces the actual behaviour of the target in the period 1967–73 is as follows:

KEN 17: FR target at quarter $t = \dfrac{\sum\limits_{i=1}^{12} M_{(t-i+1)}}{12}$

The result of the arithmetical exercise (simulation S5) is that foreign reserves would not have been less than 35 per cent above the minimum target at any time during the period 1970–73. At the end of 1973, FR would have stood at K.sh. 1860 millions; the target would have been about K.sh. 1320 millions. There would have been no need for import controls, or indeed for active Central Bank intervention to restrict the aggregate lending activity of the commercial banks.

6.3 STABILIZING THE KENYAN ECONOMY

6.31 *The Scope for Credit Expansion to the Government*

According to KEN, credit expansions to the government have only a small and temporary effect upon prices and economic activity. Their permanent effect is upon the foreign reserve position. So if the government sets itself a minimum target for the level of foreign reserves, it is a straightforward matter to calculate the maximum credit expansion that can be sustained.

A rough indication of this amount for the period 1967–73 may be obtained from the result of simulation S5 reported in the previous section: if the commercial banks had been fully loaned up at the end of the period and government had borrowed *nothing* from the monetary system, foreign reserves would have been about K.sh. 540 millions above the minimum target at the end of 1973. This suggests that there was room during the seven-year period for a credit expansion to the government of this amount – slightly less than one per cent of monetary GDP, and slightly more than the K.sh. 480 millions that the government actually borrowed from its monetary system during these years.

It is possible to make this estimate rather more precise by simulating the behaviour of foreign reserves and the minimum target (on the assumption that the commercial banks remain fully loaned up) with different ratios of ΔDA_G to Y over the period as a whole. According to KEN's simulation S6, foreign reserves would have been 43 per cent above the minimum target at the end of 1973 if no credit expansion to the government had taken place; and according to S7, reserves would have been about 7 per cent *below* the target with a steady credit expansion to the government of 1 per cent of monetary GDP. A safe guideline for the period would have been about 0.8 per cent of monetary GDP.

Now, this is not very much for a government that feels itself to be hard pressed for revenue. But even this modest figure is an exaggeration of KEN's implications about the scope for credit expansion to the Kenya government in the long run. For the estimate is specific to the years 1967–73, and in three respects these years were an exceptionally favourable time for such a credit expansion to be undertaken with safety.

First and most obviously, Kenya's reserves started the period at a level which was K.sh. 147 millions above the target, which provided the authorities with an initial bonus. If this bonus is neglected, the safe figure is reduced from 0.8 per cent to 0.6 per cent of monetary GDP.

Second, the estimate is based upon the assumption – among many others – that the demand for money in Kenya will remain as elastic in future as it proved to be during the period that has been studied. But, as D. H. Robertson has warned in his *Lectures on Economic Principles*, 'the incalculable k of the public hangs like the sword of Damocles over the head of many amiable and ambitious schemes'. If the demand for money in Kenya should shift downwards in response to accelerating inflation or for any other reason, the government would no longer be able to borrow 0.6 per cent of monetary GDP from the banking system without permanently endangering the reserve target. So the estimate depends among other things on the assumption that the government does not allow significant domestic inflation to continue.

But third and most seriously of all, if no inflation had in fact occurred during the period, the estimate of the scope for safe credit expansion would not have been 0.6 per cent of monetary GDP, but approximately zero. In practice, Kenya's foreign receipts and nominal income rose during the period studied here at an *increasing* rate, mainly because of accelerating increases in export prices. The fact that the minimum target for foreign reserves was defined as a three-year moving average of imports necessarily ensured that this target would rise at a *lower* rate. But this is not a stable situation in the long run: if the rate of increase of foreign receipts and nominal income were to be stabilized, the rate of increase of the minimum reserve target would catch up and the scope for safe credit expansion would disappear.

In other words, given the minimum target for foreign reserves that is stipulated in the Central Bank of Kenya Act, the only safe rule for credit expansion to the Kenya government in the long run is that *none should be undertaken*. Any systematic infringement of this rule is bound to lead to balance of payments 'crises'.

However, this rather rigorous conclusion must be qualified in two respects. In the first place, the conclusion concerns only credit expansions to the government in particular forms (such as Treasury Bill issues and direct advances from the Central Bank) which do not impair the capacity of the banking system to make credit available to the private sector. Such 'short term' borrowing was in fact how the Kenya government obtained its credit from the monetary system during the years 1967–73, but it need not remain so. If instead the government was prepared to borrow on the same terms as the private sector (or to make room for its short term borrowing by imposing increasingly severe liquid asset requirements upon the commercial banks), some room for safe borrowing from the monetary system would indeed be created.

In the second place, the conclusion does not of course rule out the possibility of government using credit expansions as an anti-cyclical device, with any borrowing in the recession being fully repaid in the recovery phase of the cycle. The difficulties here are of a practical kind: but they are illustrated rather dramatically by the eighteen-month delay between the Kenyan authorities' decision to borrow in 1970 and the impact of this decision upon the economy. Since model KEN suggests that budgetary policy has a relatively small effect upon economic activity at the best of times, the value of a counter-cyclical policy – even if it could be successfully undertaken – might well be fairly modest.

6.32   *Stabilizing Prices through Exchange Rate Policy*

In model KEN the behaviour of domestic prices is governed almost entirely by import and export prices in foreign currency terms, and by the effective exchange rate. The Nairobi cost of living indices rose between the end of 1969 and the end of 1973 by 31 per cent. According to KEN this was due almost entirely to a 36 per cent rise in import prices and a 33 per cent rise in export prices in the same period. But in the model, the effective exchange rate could have been used in principle as an instrument of policy to maintain exact stability in the equilibrium level of domestic prices. So it is of some interest to calculate the effective rate changes which would have been necessary to achieve this target.

Model KEN has been used to generate two estimates of such an exchange rate policy – first, on the assumption that no credit expansion to the government took place (S8) and second, on the assumption that this credit expansion proceeded at a rate equal to one per cent of monetary GDP (S9). As might be expected on the basis of the discussion in the previous section of this chapter, the target level of foreign reserves is almost exactly maintained in S8, whereas in S9 reserves fall 45 per cent below the target by the end of 1973. So it is the results of S8 only which are of practical interest here. S8's exchange rate policy is illustrated in Figure 6.4, together with the actual behaviour of the Kenya shilling's effective exchange rate. (The third policy which is illustrated in Figure 6.4, namely S10, will be explained shortly.) .

This diagram shows that the exchange rate policy needed to ensure a stable equilibrium level of domestic prices was almost exactly the policy that the Kenyan authorities actually pursued, up to the beginning of 1970. But from this point onwards domestic price stability would have required a steady appreciation of the effective exchange rate, whereas the policy actually followed (as described in Chapter 4) was to maintain this rate, with some fluctuations from 1971 onwards, at an approximately constant level.

It is one thing to calculate with the wisdom of hindsight the exchange rate changes that would have been necessary to maintain price stability: it is a very different matter to indicate how these changes might have been determined at the

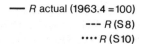

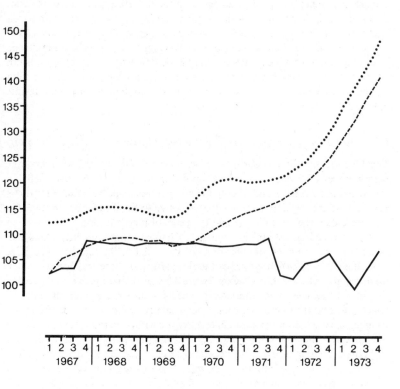

FIGURE 6.4 *Alternative Exchange Rate Policies*

time by the Kenyan authorities. But the discussion of model MFF in Chapter 2 suggests that a similar outcome would have resulted with a perfectly flexible exchange rate system, given a stable rate of domestic credit expansion. So model KEN has been used to calculate, in S10, how a perfectly flexible exchange rate for the Kenya shilling would have behaved with a steady credit expansion to the government equal to one per cent of monetary GDP. As Figure 6.4 shows, the exchange rate changes under such a system would have been similar to, although not exactly the same as, those which were necessary to maintain domestic price stability.

It would be difficult in an economy such as Kenya's to devise a practical system that would approximate the behaviour of the theoretical construct of a perfectly flexible exchange rate system. And such a system would certainly have been against both the spirit and the letter of Kenya's obligations in the early

1970s as a member of the International Monetary Fund. But there was nothing in these obligations to prevent the Kenyan authorities from taking decisions from 1971 onwards to bring about roughly those changes that were necessary to stabilize the equilibrium level of domestic prices. Indeed, a wide variety of countries – including Malaysia, Kuwait, Belgium and Japan among those with which Kenya trades on a significant scale – took exchange rate decisions between 1971 and 1973 which would have resulted in the Kenyan context in effective exchange rate behaviour almost identical to that of S8. So domestic price stability was not only a theoretical possibility: it could also have been achieved in practice, with careful management and perhaps a bit of luck, and without offending against any of Kenya's international obligations.

6.33 *Maintaining a High Level of Economic Activity*

This final section will necessarily be rather more speculative than what has gone before, since KEN does not formally model fluctuations in economic activity. But something must be said, if only for completeness, and because fluctuations in economic activity may reasonably be expected to be more serious in Kenya in the future than they were in the first ten years of independence.

It was argued on theoretical grounds in Chapter 2 that such fluctuations can occur only when prices are inflexible, so that a fall in the rate of expenditure upon domestically produced goods (and in particular those that are sold upon domestic markets, which in Chapter 2 were labelled [D]) leads to some tendency for firms to reduce the quantity which they produce rather than the price at which they sell. If this is accepted, it follows that governments can do two things to minimize fluctuations in economic activity. The first is to prevent downward fluctuations in the *equilibrium* price of [D]; and the second is to take whatever steps they can to ensure that the *actual* prices of [D] are as flexible as possible.

Now, if the price of imports rises while that of exports falls, the use of the exchange rate to stabilize P_A will entail a downward movement in the equilibrium price of [D] and may therefore be harmful to the level of economic activity. But in Kenya, between 1969 and 1973, import and export prices rose at roughly the same rate. Stabilizing P_A , as in simulation S8, would have entailed much smaller downward movements in the equilibrium price of [D] than the 10 per cent decline which model KEN implies actually took place during 1972 as a result of the government's expenditure-restricting policies. It therefore seems unlikely that Kenya would have paid a high price in this period, in terms of fluctuations in economic activity, for a stable domestic price level.

Furthermore the direct controls upon imports and prices which were introduced in 1972 seem likely to have positively harmed the level of activity. For firms may reasonably be expected to be more reluctant to reduce their prices if they fear that they may be prevented subsequently from putting them up once again; and an interuption to the flow of imported raw materials is likely to cause some firms to operate at levels below those at which they would otherwise choose to produce. So such measures not only affect the efficiency with which resources are allocated in the economy: they are *also* likely to lead in the long run to a lower average level of economic activity.

It seems reasonable to conclude that the most promising approach to maintaining a high level of economic activity in Kenya would be the avoidance of measures such as those with which the authorities felt obliged at the end of 1971 to remedy a balance of payments crisis. And this, according to model KEN, is easily done. All that is required is the avoidance of any reliance upon privileged borrowing from the monetary system.

Part 3

CONCLUSION

Economics is not nearly as much of a science as the free use of allegedly accurate figures would seem to indicate. On the other hand, there is no reason to conclude that there cannot be or is no theory at all. The belief, that we have to get more and more data, make more and more descriptions before we can formulate valid theories is entirely mistaken. A theory means a commitment and in scientific life that is exactly what is wanted. When new facts come to light and new interpretations are needed, a new situation can arise. This may then call for abandoning the old views and for making a new decision.

Oskar Morgenstern

7 *Macroeconomic Policy and Theory in an African Setting*

An increasing reliance on textbooks or their equivalent [is] an invariable concomitant of the emergence of a first paradigm in any field of science.

T. S. Kuhn

7.1 ALTERNATIVE ASSESSMENTS OF THE KENYAN EXPERIENCE

7.11 *Introduction*

Part 2 examined in some detail a relatively short period of Kenya's history, concentrating exclusively upon what have been defined in this book as the objectives and instruments of stabilization policy. In some ways, the fact that the study ends with the year 1973 is unfortunate. For in general the concerns which this study has investigated were seen as much less pressing by the Kenyan authorities before 1973 than they have since become.

But in other ways this has been an advantage. For precisely because economic stabilization took second place to long run concerns such as growth, employment, and the distribution of income in Kenya during the period this was essentially a time of experiment – a time when the constraints of the colonial period would be progressively abandoned, and the possibilities of an independent, national stabilization policy would be explored in a trial and error manner. Sometimes these experiments were deliberate; sometimes they were imposed upon the Kenyan authorities by outside events and circumstances.

In the years 1972–73 there was a concerted attempt in the Kenya Treasury and Central Bank to draw some lessons from the record of stabilization policy, in preparation for the publication of a new Development Plan for the years 1974–78. This reappraisal could be conducted in a relatively calm atmosphere. For between the middle of 1972 and the middle of 1973, inflation in Kenya was proceeding at a comparatively moderate rate; the balance of payments was once more in healthy surplus after the crisis of 1971; and there was no longer any perception of a seriously depressed level of economic activity, as there had been in 1969–70. Two aspects of this reappraisal are worth examination here, as it appeared in government publications and statements of policy.

7.12   *The Balance of Payments*

In the first place, there was a recognition that the severe import restrictions of 1972 were having serious distorting effects upon the domestic economy. The Central Bank argued in its 1972 Annual Report that

> Import licensing and exchange controls may help to prevent over-importation and a drain on foreign reserves, but in the Bank's view it would be unwise to rely too much on these restrictions. In its capacity as Kenya's exchange controller, the Bank has a daily exposure to the weaknesses and inefficiencies of these techniques as a permanent solution to managing the balance of payments.

A similar view was expressed by the Minister for Finance, Mwai Kibaki, in his budget speeches in 1972 and 1973 and a relaxation of import restrictions was indeed commenced in the middle of 1973. The new Development Plan which was published at the end of the year noted that 'some kind of import restraint' would be required if its balance of payments projections were to be achieved in the years 1974–78; but the Plan made it clear that direct controls were not seen as a suitable restraining weapon:

> Hopefully, the rise in international prices will lead to voluntary cutbacks in amount. If this does not occur to a sufficient extent, Government will have to evoke other import-limiting policies, which may involve taxation, monetary policy, etc.

The new Development Plan was slightly less optimistic than its predecessor had been about the scope for government borrowing from the banking system. It proposed an annual ceiling of K.sh. 360 millions (at 1973–74 prices), and an average annual level of K.sh. 300 millions between 1974 and 1978. This was about 2 per cent of the 1973–74 level of monetary GDP at current market prices.

There was, indeed, a recognition that government borrowing from the banking system and the behaviour of the balance of payments were connected. But the Kenyan authorities' assessment of this connection is in striking contrast to the one that has been put forward in this book. For according to model KEN, a fiscal guideline that allowed such borrowing to continue at any positive level, let alone 2 per cent of monetary GDP, was a prescription for a balance of payments crisis. If KEN's lesson is valid, it is a lesson that had not been learned.

7.13   *Inflation*

The moderate inflation of 1971–72 and its acceleration in 1973 presented the authorities with a new problem – a problem which became increasingly serious as the drafting of the new Development Plan proceeded. The Plan's discussion of this problem was brief, but unambiguous:

The Government is determined to keep inflation within tolerable limits. This task will be the more difficult because world inflation will be transmitted to Kenya through the prices of imports and exports. However, ... the increases in domestic prices can be held at a lower percentage than those of the rest of the world. ... This will be done by vigorous application of monetary policy.

In the past, the Government has relied on price controls. ... [But] because price controls distort the allocation of resources and cause the wrong goods to be produced, the Government does not intend to adopt them in the regular arsenal of anti-inflation weapons. It will, rather, rely on traditional instruments of monetary and fiscal policy.

The only mention of the exchange rate contained in the Plan was a statement that Kenya would, 'in consultation with the Partner States of the East African Community', seek to maintain 'an appropriate value for the Kenya shilling'. In practice this meant an approximately stable effective exchange rate. Indeed this target was to be formalized in 1975 when Kenya pegged its currency to the Special Drawing Right – a unit that had become by this time an average of the major trading currencies.

Once again, the contrast with KEN's implications is striking. Although they were clearly concerned to restrain domestic inflation, the Kenyan authorities were committing themselves not to use the only instrument that could effectively achieve this. They were to rely instead upon instruments which could have at most a transitory influence.

This criticism should not be misinterpreted. It is not being suggested here that the Kenyan authorities necessarily *should* try to maintain complete domestic price stability. In the early 1970s there were several reasons why a sharp, temporary inflation might have been seen as a good thing. For example, it was widely believed that there were chronic disequilibria in Kenyan labour markets, and that these disequilibria resulted in large measure from a rigid structure of money wage rates inherited from the colonial period. To the extent that this diagnosis of Kenya's employment problem was valid, a sharp inflation would have done much to cure it. But this kind of argument supports a deliberate and controlled inflation only. It does not support a policy of allowing the price level in Kenya to be dictated for ever by the Treasuries and Central Banks of other countries.

Nor does it seem likely that the Kenyan authorities would have chosen this latter policy if they had believed there to be any viable alternative. Mwai Kibaki wrote in the preface to the new Plan that 'we have already sorted out those areas over which we Kenyans exercise control, from those which depend on events and decisions made elsewhere in the world'. The argument here is simply that this judgment was wrong in one important respect: the domestic inflation rate *could* have been controlled by the Kenyan authorities, even in the turbulent world of the early 1970s.

7.2 ALTERNATIVE PARADIGMS

Why is it that the conclusions in this book, drawn from Kenya's experience in the first ten years of independence are so different, in these important respects, from those that were drawn by the Kenyan authorities? Clearly, it is not because the authorities were not studying the record for empirical answers to questions about how the economy worked: they were doing so with great thoroughness. Nor is the answer that the data used in this study differ from what were available to the authorities. Instead, the answer is that the same data were being studied from a different perspective and with different techniques.

The techniques of applied macroeconomics which the Kenyan authorities were using to investigate the empirical record were those suggested as appropriate by model ODM and its various extensions. This model is built around a relationship – the multiplier – of which no trace can be found in the Kenyan experience. And it obscures two relationships which are central to model MFF – the relationship between domestic credit expansion and foreign reserves and the relationship between the exchange rate and the equilibrium level of domestic prices. These two relationships do not emerge *directly* from a simple examination of macroeconomic data. But they do appear clearly in the Kenyan record when they are searched for with the aid of model MFF. So the theoretical model or 'paradigm' in terms of which one approaches the data has an important part to play in determining what one finds there.

Now on reading Chapter 2 some readers may have felt that it was exaggerating the differences between the two simple theoretical models. After all, they contain similar sorts of relationships, and they are built around the same accounting identities. It should therefore be a relatively straightforward matter to combine them in some sort of compromise. And indeed it is. At the frontiers of research in economic theory in recent years there have been several attempts to fill in some of the gaps in the simple Keynesian model of an open economy, such as the wealth effect, the supply and demand for 'bonds' and the demand for money; the implications of the model when developed along these lines have a great deal in common with those of MFF.

There was, therefore, an element of caricature in Chapter 2. But there was a reason for it. For it should now be clear that the models upon which different schools of thought take their stand, upon which conventional wisdoms are founded and from which applied economists derive their techniques of analysis, are not large models containing many behavioural equations, whose precise implications can only be distilled with the aid of computers or higher mathematics. Instead, they are simple models such as those contained in Chapter 2. They are the sort of models that are found in the introductory textbooks from which each generation of economists learns the outline of the subject.

7.3   AN ALTERNATIVE APPROACH
TO MACROECONOMICS

So it is of critical importance *which* simple model is chosen as a starting point in the teaching of macroeconomics. Upon this choice will depend the perceptions of a generation of practising economists – the questions they ask of empirical data, the way in which they seek answers to these questions, and the specific answers

they obtain. Upon these will depend in turn the conventional wisdoms of decision makers in matters of stabilization policy. Finally, upon these conventional
wisdoms will depend in large measure what actually happens in particular
economies – whether inflation is controlled or not; whether fluctuations in
economic activity are large or small, encouraged or discouraged; whether the
balance of payments is 'strong', or staggers instead from crisis to crisis; whether
administrative controls over prices, wages, imports, capital flows and so on
appear to become indispensable and so spread throughout the economy;
whether a country becomes so deeply in debt to foreign creditors that it loses the
freedom to make its own decisions about the objectives it pursues.

There are of course many other matters, even in the relatively narrow arena of
economic policy, which governments may judge more important than these. But
enough should now have been said to convince the reader that the choice of
model in the teaching of macroeconomics, with which this book has been concerned, is an important one.

At the end of the first part of this book it was argued that if the student is to
understand contemporary debate about stabilization policy he must be familiar
with more than one macroeconomic model. There is no need to withdraw that
conclusion. But it is necessary to start somewhere, and I must now come off the
fence and say firmly where I think the teaching of macroeconomics should start.

In the Kenyan context, the answer is clear. The prevailing approach to
macroeconomics teaching, based upon ODM and its various extensions, is not
only misleading but dangerously so. It serves not to enlighten the student about
the world in which he lives but to obscure his understanding of it. It provides a
perspective which prevents him from perceiving relationships which exist, and
which matter. On the other hand, a model like MFF is no more complicated; it is
aesthetically superior, as suggested in Chapter 2; and it is wholly consistent with
the Kenyan experience.

This conclusion has been based upon the record of a single country in a very
brief period of its history. It seems unlikely, however, that Kenya is unique in the
relevant respects among the open economies of the world.

Index